THE ENVIRONMENTAL CASE FOR BREXIT

The recent Brexit debates present leaving the European Union largely as a threat to environmental protection, and to environmental law. This exciting and important new work argues that Brexit represents a real opportunity for environmental protection in the United Kingdom, freeing it from a pan-European framework not necessarily fit for UK domestic purposes. Central to the argument is the belief that environmental protection, in the United Kingdom, can most effectively be pursued through established domestic institutions, looking inwards at 'local' challenges and outwards at more global ones, all the while drawing on considerable historical experience. The book is designed to address rather than dismiss those concerns raised by environmental lawyers after the outcome of the referendum. Provocative and compelling, it offers an alternative vision of the UK environmental law framework outside of the European Union.

The Environmental Case for Brexit

A Socio-legal Perspective

Ben Pontin

·HART·

OXFORD · LONDON · NEW YORK · NEW DELHI · SYDNEY

HART PUBLISHING

Bloomsbury Publishing Plc

Kemp House, Chawley Park, Cumnor Hill, Oxford, OX2 9PH, UK

HART PUBLISHING, the Hart/Stag logo, BLOOMSBURY and the Diana logo are
trademarks of Bloomsbury Publishing Plc

First published in Great Britain 2019

A catalogue record for this book is available from the British Library.

Library of Congress Cataloging-in-Publication data

Names: Pontin, Ben, author.

Title: The environmental case for Brexit : a socio-legal perspective / Ben Pontin.

Description: Oxford, UK ; Portland, Oregon : Hart Publishing, 2019. |
Includes bibliographical references and index.

Identifiers: LCCN 2018050679 (print) | LCCN 2018051115 (ebook) |
ISBN 9781509920907 (EPub) | ISBN 9781509920891 (hardback)

Subjects: LCSH: Environmental law—Great Britain. | European Union—
Great Britain. | Law—Great Britain—European influences. | BISAC: LAW / Environmental.

Classification: LCC KD3372 (ebook) | LCC KD3372 .P658 2019 (print) |
DDC 344.4104/6—dc23

LC record available at https://lccn.loc.gov/2018050679

ISBN: HB: 978-1-50992-089-1
        ePDF: 978-1-50992-091-4
        ePub: 978-1-50992-090-7

Typeset by Compuscript Ltd, Shannon
Printed and bound in Great Britain by CPI Group (UK) Ltd, Croydon CR0 4YY

To find out more about our authors and books visit www.hartpublishing.co.uk.
Here you will find extracts, author information, details of forthcoming events
and the option to sign up for our newsletters.

Preface

THIS BOOK IS based on lectures and seminars delivered within the Environmental Law and Justice LLB module at Cardiff School of Law and Politics. In the seminars in particular, and the coursework associated with them, the students have been discussing the issues addressed in this book, shaping its content. I would like to thank students for entering into the spirit of these experiments in 'teaching-led research'.

Some students have made a special contribution, which I would like to acknowledge. For the students who took the course shortly after the EU Referendum (academic year 2016–17), these are: Natalie Cernuschi, Juliette Eden, Emily Edwards, Danielle Futcher, Dimitri bin Rosli, Shannon Ryan Creagh, Sophie Tremlin, Jack Woods.

For especially helpful contributions this academic year (2017–18), I would like to acknowledge: Yahya Al-Qaq, Timothy Gong, Marina Soares Ingles, Jade Jones, Jack Mitchell and Charles Wilson.

For comments on earlier drafts of opening material, I am extremely grateful to Liz Fisher, Val Fogleman and Nigel Haigh. I would also like to thank Ambreena Manji for encouragement – to the extent that any was needed – to use the law jobs theory in this book, especially as it appears in the work of William Twining, with whom Ambreena has worked closely. William was my Jurisprudence tutor at University College London, during my LLM; I have always wanted to thank him for being so brilliantly inspirational.

I am indebted to my family, especially my wife, Elspeth, for taking good care of us all, as I have concentrated on this book.

Last, but not least, I would like to acknowledge the extremely helpful team at Hart – thanks Tom, Catherine and everyone!

Ben Pontin
Cardiff
December 2018

Contents

1

Introduction

THIS BOOK EXPLORES the environmental case for Britain's withdrawal from the European Union (EU). It does so against the backdrop of widespread concern that environment law and, crucially, the environment itself will suffer as a consequence of Britain's exiting the EU. The environment has made the 'journey to the centre stage' of the EU,[1] such that nearly all areas of domestic regulatory law concerning the environment are connected with the EU acquis to a greater or lesser extent.[2] What will happen to regulatory law when Britain withdraws from the EU? What will happen to the environment? One worry is that the rigour of EU-derived domestic legislation that is retained ('retained law') will be relaxed to boost the economy. Another is 'zombie law', where retained law is stripped of the jurisdiction of the European Commission and European Court of Justice, giving only an illusion of environmental protection.[3] Mindful of this, commentators lean towards a Brexit that is as 'soft' as possible, by which substantive EU law is retained and backed by a system of governance (especially concerning monitoring and enforcement) which replicates that of the EU.[4]

These concerns are reasonable and sincere, and the purpose of my book is not to impugn them. Rather, the purpose is to situate anxiety

---

[1] N Haigh, *EU Environmental Policy: Its Journey to the Centre Stage* (Routledge 2016).

[2] For 'gaps' in the EU acquis, eg in respect of nuclear power and soil protection, see L Kramer, 'EU Environmental Law and Policy Over the Last 25 Years – Good or Bad for the UK?' (2013) 25 *Environmental Law and Management* 48, 52–53.

[3] A Jordan, Evidence (Q5), House of Lords European Union and Energy Select Committee, *Inquiry on the Potential Implications of Brexit on Environmental Policy*, 20 July 2016.

[4] eg C Hilson, 'The Impact of Brexit on the Environment: Exploring the Dynamics of a Complex Relationship' (2018) 7 *Transnational Environmental Law* 89; C Burns, V Gravey and A Jordan, *UK Environmental Policy Post-Brexit: A Risk Assessment* (Friends of the Earth 2018). See too the 'risk tracker' and wider contributions of Greener UK alliance (www.greeneruk.org). Cf the emphasis on the opportunities for 'home grown' developments in the law after Brexit, eg J Thornton and R Macrory, 'An Environmentally Ambitious Brexit', *Demos Quarterly*, 20 June 2017; R Lee, 'Always Keep a Hold of Nurse: British Environmental Law and Exit from the European Union' (2017) 29 *Journal of Environmental Law* 155.

about the future of environmental law outside of the EU in a broader socio-legal context, taking into account the historical development of the law (both British and EU) and the practical impact of formal law on the physical environment. The themes of formal law, historical influence and 'real world impact' come together particularly well in Karl Llewellyn's 'law jobs theory',[5] and it is this that provides the theoretical framework for my study. According to this theory, law is a 'way' of facilitating the doing of jobs that are necessary for a society to survive and to flourish, including shaping and reflecting societal values, creating incentives to do things better, channelling behaviour to minimise disputes and resolving disputes that arise. Environmental law cuts across each area of this job description, yet the theory has attracted surprisingly little attention in environmental law scholarship.[6] Britain's withdrawal from the EU is a timely opportunity to begin to make good this gap in the literature. How will Britain's departure from the EU impact on the doing of 'environmental law jobs'? Will it really create weaknesses that need addressing? Might it create greater opportunities for these jobs to be done well?

The law jobs theory connects strongly with the present subject matter, because of the narrative of there being a 'British way' of doing environmental protection that was dominant when Britain entered the Community.[7] This narrative emerged in response to the internationalisation of environmental politics, culminating in the United Nations Conference on the Human Environment, in Stockholm in 1972. It operated (as the saying goes) both as a sword and as a shield: as a sword in the sense that it helped position Britain as a global leader in international environmental policy and law; as a shield in demarcating a territory for exclusive control through domestic institutions. As Nigel Haigh pointed out in his early history of Britain's relationship with

---

[5] K Llewellyn and A Hoebel, *The Cheyenne Way: Conflict and Case Law in Primitive Jurisprudence* (WS Hein and Co 1941) ch 10 and ch 11; K Llewellyn, 'Law and the Social Sciences – Especially Sociology' (1949) 62 *Harvard Law Review* 1286. See further W Twining, *Karl Llewellyn and the American Legal Realist Movement*, 2nd edn (Cambridge University Press 2014) (especially ch 8).

[6] Cf L Kotze, *Global Environmental Governance: Law and Regulation for the 21st Century* (Edward Elgar 2012) 155–58. Another work of Llewellyn's (*The Bramble Bush*) is mentioned in E Fisher, *Environmental Law: A Very Short Introduction* (Oxford University Press 2017) 122, 124. Fisher develops this is the context of 'environmental legal education' in E Fisher, 'Back to Basics: Thinking About the Craft of Environmental Law Scholarship' in O Pedersen, *Perspectives on Environmental Law Scholarship* (Cambridge University Press 2018).

[7] E Ashby et al, *Pollution: Nuisance or Nemesis* (HMSO 1972) 58.

EU environmental law,[8] the emphasis on a national way of doing law in this field distinguished Britain from the countries who invented the European Economic Community. The founders (hereafter EU-6) embraced 'some kind of supra-nationalism'.[9] Whilst they too had their own ways of doing environmental law, they were more willing than Britain to treat environmental law (in Ludwig Kramer's words) as 'virgin law'.[10] Britain, by contrast, emphasised its embeddedness in national heritage. It considered relinquishing of the established crafts of environmental law shaped by centuries of experience to a new juris-diction as unnecessary and irresponsible. I examine the merits of that stance and its relevance to articulating a positive environmental case for Brexit. Is recourse to a national way in Britain the responsible position to adopt moving forward, as Britain exits the EU? If so, how can that be reconciled with other European countries' continuing embracing of a greater degree of 'supra-nationalism'?

A helpful starting point in introducing the British way as a norma-tive tool is provided by the speech of Peter Walker, the British Secretary of State for the Environment, at the Stockholm Conference.[11] Britain, he said, had the world's most established regulatory laws regarding industrial pollution control and nature conservation, the foundations of which were laid by Parliament at Westminster in Victorian times. These laws coexisted alongside medieval-originating common law and Scots law conceptions of property in land, giving expression to the ethics of the 'good steward' and the 'good neighbour', to constitute a dynamic mix of 'public law' and 'private law', written and unwrit-ten. The enforcement of this law by executive bodies and individuals brought visible benefits, such as cleaner industrial processes, prevention

---

[8] N Haigh, *EEC Environmental Policy and Britain: An Essay and a Handbook* (ENDS Data Services 1984) (hereinafter *Essay and Handbook*).

[9] ibid 2. The term 'EU-6' refers to the six current Member States who were found-ing members of the European Economic Community: Belgium, France, Germany, Italy, Luxembourg, and the Netherlands.

[10] L Kramer, 'Law in an Open Society' (1989) 1 *Journal of Environmental Law* 1, 3. Kramer has recently commented on the impact of expansion of the EU, in terms of Member States without a pre-EU history of environmental policy and law being now in the majority: Kramer, n 2, 50.

[11] Rt Hon Peter Walker, 'Britain and the Environment', World Conference on Envi-ronment and Development, Stockholm, 6 June 1972. For a contemporary summary, see S Johnson, *The Politics of the Environment: The British Experience* (Tom Stacey 1972) 216–19. For background to the cross-party and 'home nations' British delegation, see M Holdgate, *Penguins and Mandarins: The Memoirs of Martin Holdgate* (The Memoir Club 2003) 190–97 (the delegation comprised ministerial representatives of Wales and Scotland, plus the Shadow Environment Secretary Tony Crosland and the Chair of the Royal Commission on Environmental Pollution (Eric Ashby)).

of waste, conservation of flora and fauna, and the protection of bucolic countryside accessible to all.

Walker was situating the British vision of international environmental policy and law within a Westphalian paradigm geared around mutual recognition of national sovereignty.[12] This approach was popular across the British political spectrum, for it appeared to reconcile the established Westminster system of 'responsible government' with an internationalism that appealed to emergent environmental activists. Thus few would have objected to the sentiments of Stanley Johnson, who commented that 'Peter Walker's speech that afternoon was the culmination of an effort which began with the Alkali Acts of the mid nineteenth century or even, some might say, earlier still'.[13] Johnson added that 'We [Britain] probably knew more about environmental planning and management than anyone else'.[14] The 'we' in this setting had a broad meaning, referring to the '50 million volunteers' (ie British subjects) on whose efforts the country could count when it came to inspirationally effective ways of protecting the environment.[15]

This narrative led Britain's political leaders to be wary of the Community's assumption of competence in the field of the environment. Aware that the Commission was drafting a programme of environmental action under a Council mandate given to it in 1971,[16] Peter Walker instructed civil servants to take 'a positive part in the discussions as they develop, to influence the Community's thinking',[17] yet 'guard against making pollution measures obligatory, in the cause of harmonisation, *in circumstances where they are not called for in practical terms*'.[18]

According to Martin Holdgate – the official who headed the Environmental Protection Group within the Department of

---

[12] Cf Sweden, whose delegation urged a more supra-national world order: Holdgate, n 11, 190.

[13] Johnson, n 11, 216. The reference to the Alkali Acts is to Acts of 1863, 1868, 1874, 1881. See also Holdgate, n 11, 202.

[14] Johnson, n 11, 222.

[15] D Stevenson et al, *Organisation and Youth: 50 million Volunteers* (HMSO 1972) xiv. For an influential sociological comparative analysis of the importance of civil society in Britain, see B Badie and P Birnbaum, *The Sociology of the State*, trans A Goldhammer (University of Chicago Press 1983). On the importance of civil society to environmental protection in the comparative setting of Britain and Germany, see C Knill, *The Europeanisation of National Administrations* (Cambridge University Press 2001) 74.

[16] Commission SEC(71)2616 final (22 July 1971). See further L Kramer, *EEC Treaty and Environmental Protection* (Sweet & Maxwell 1990) 1.

[17] Department of Environment Memorandum 1971, 'Implications for DOE of UK Membership of the Common Market' (National Archives, MT 134/27).

[18] ibid (emphasis added).

Environment – the phrase 'practical terms' meant dealing with trans-boundary pollution and trade, but little else; as a general rule, 'it should be left to countries to protect their own environments'.[19] This was the message of the text of the Stockholm Declaration, and the expectation was that pollution would continue to be controlled, and nature conserved, in accordance with the British way.

In what follows I revisit that expectation, with particular reference to literature published on the cusp of the Single European Act 1986, when the Community's environmental competence received an explicit formal treaty mandate. A key work in this respect is Nigel Haigh's *Essay and Handbook*.[20] The 'Essay' part of the work situates Community law in the context of historic developments in domestic environmental law and emerging international law. The 'Handbook' analyses the practical impact on domestic provision of Community interventions in the fields of water, waste, air, nature conservation and others. In this respect Haigh draws on discussions with officials within the Department of Environment, thus adopting an 'empirical' approach. This was thought necessary because of the absence of formal signs of Community impact: Britain, when Haigh was writing, was operating within the pre-Community framework of the Environment White Paper of 1970 (as it remained until *This Common Inheritance*, in 1990).[21]

The value of Haigh's approach lies in its attention to detail. Haigh's chief finding within the empirical ('Handbook') part of the analysis is as follows:

> With the benefit of hindsight ... the passing by the British Parliament of the European Communities Act 1972 was [a] significant step that has changed the way an important part of British environmental policy is now thought about, enunciated and ultimately is even put into practice.[22]

This sets an agenda for my work. How did the domestic position change as a consequence of Community – and more recently EU – membership? Has change been for the better? Haigh's *Essay and Handbook* received a favourable response from Eric Ashby, one of the main critics of Community environmental interventions and the chief advocate of the British way.[23] But what significance should be attached to that?

---

[19] Holdgate, n 11,190.

[20] Haigh, *Essay and Handbook*, n 8.

[21] Her Majesty's Government, *The Protection of the Environment: The Fight Against Pollution*, Cm 4373 (HMSO 1970); Her Majesty's Government, *This Common Inheritance: Britain's Environment Strategy*, Cm 1200 (HMSO 1990).

[22] Haigh, *Essay and Handbook*, n 8, 1.

[23] E Ashby, 'Between Brussels and Westminster', *Nature*, 26 April 1984, 802–03.

I argue that experience of EU membership has largely vindicated doubts about a novel supranational competence expressed by advocates of the British way on entry to the Community. The fundamentals of the British way paradigm as a sword and shield remain valid today. The responsible approach to environmental policy, law and practice in Britain (and its wider global relationships) is independent of EU institutions.

The structure of the book is as follows. Chapter 2 elaborates on the British way of environmental protection, drawing upon political science as well as law disciplinary literature, and using the law jobs theory as an organising concept for doing so. The law jobs theory is particularly helpful because it is descriptive *and* normative. It highlights the institutional conditions under which (environmental) law jobs are well done. The chapter anticipates criticisms of the British way and my argument that it is relevant post-Brexit. Some of these involve a more jaundiced (or less rose-tinted) perception of the British way as Britain entered the Community, whilst others address the existential issue that, rightly or wrongly, the British way has not survived membership of the EU and devolution. The chapter also introduces the 'case studies' through which the environmental case for Brexit is articulated.

Case study is method by which Llewellyn and Hoebel illuminated the functionality of Cheyenne law-ways, and it is also the approach of political scientists studying European integration noted above.[24] My book revisits areas examined by Haigh's *Essay and Handbook*, namely, waste, water quality, air quality and nature conservation. These reflect some of the diversity of the challenges tackled by EU environmental law. They are also widely associated with the *benefits* of EU membership.[25] Britain's environment in these fields, so the argument goes, is 'getting better', and that is testimony to the benefits of the EU acquis, and the desirability of mirroring EU law as far as possible after Brexit.

These fields are also selected because of the existence of thorough contemporary records of domestic environmental 'performance' when the EU journey began. Thus it is possible to compare with some precision the environment 'on the ground' as Britain prepares to leave with that when it entered. Against that backdrop, the 'getting better' notion is rather problematic. Per capita production of waste is considerably

---

[24] See especially A Jordan, *Europeanization of British Environmental Policy: A Departmental Perspective* (Palgrave Macmillan 2002) 14–17. See too Knill, n 15; and R Wurzel, *Environmental Policy-Making in Britain, Germany and the European Union* (Manchester University Press 2006).

[25] In particular Burns et al, n 4; and Hilson, n 4.

greater than that on entry, whilst biodiversity has declined. Rivers are broadly of the quality they were half a century ago. Only in the field of air pollution can it be said that Britain is leaving the EU in ruder health than it entered. Britain's environment thus arguably has not largely got better, but that does not mean that there are not positive achievements to reflect on, in terms of the contribution of EU law (relative to the British way).

This leads on to the issue of apportioning the relative impact on the environment of the British way and EU law. It is notoriously hard to attribute a causal connection between law and practice on the ground in any field.[26] In the present field, the causal challenge is asymmetrical vis-à-vis the British way and EU law. By that I mean that it is easier to attribute developments in environmental quality in Britain over recent decades to domestic provision over EU law, for three reasons. First, EU law largely focuses on public law responses to environmental problems, in which competent national executive bodies are required to achieve the objectives of EU law. Thus EU law cannot claim credit for improvements resulting from private law initiatives, which are an integral part of the British way.

Second, the emphasis on formal legal prescription of what a state must do (or achieve) within the EU law means that it cannot claim credit for improvements lying outside law's *requirements* – it does not 'own' any 'goodwill' and 'voluntarism' that is responsible for the environment being in the state that it is.[27]

Third, the British way is an evolutionary process rooted years, decades and even centuries prior to Britain's entry to the Community. In the field of waste, for example, when Britain entered the Community the British Government estimated that the quantity and complexity of waste would continue to grow into the 1980s, as a consequence of the end of post-war rationing and the policies of 'consumerism' promoted by Conservative and Labour administrations from the mid 1950s. Policies and laws in the 1970s would bear fruit in reduced waste in the future. In the field of air quality, the smoke control areas enabled under the

---

[26] '[A]sserting that a law has particular effects is one thing. Demonstrating that it, in fact, has these consequences ... is quite another.' WA Bogart, *Consequences: The Impact of Law and Its Complexity* (University Toronto Press 2002) 84. See, in a Brexit context, Hilson, n 4.

[27] This opens out on to Kramer's important point that the EU lacks any central media service capable of nurturing 'cultural affinity' to the jurisdiction, comparable to those of Member States: L Kramer, *Focus on European Environmental Law*, 2nd edn (Sweet & Maxwell) 8.

Clean Air Act 1956 were designed to be implemented incrementally over many decades, as cleaner alternatives to the traditional 'open, pokeable companionable domestic fire' became available. The seeds of this legislation were clean air Bills put before Parliament in Victorian times.

Thus, by way of an overview of the case studies, and beginning with waste – the focus of chapter 3 – Britain is leaving the EU as one of the least wasteful (or most waste preventative) in terms of municipal waste among the EU-9 (the Member States when Britain joined).[28] The chapter attributes this to a significant extent to the British way in this field as it evolved during and after the Second World War. An alternative argument is that Britain's achievements are the result of the 'waste hierarchy' (with prevention at the top, safe disposal at the bottom, and re-use and recycling in between) introduced by the Waste Framework Directive of 1991, and thus exiting the EU is a risk. One problem with this is that, until recently, the emphasis of the European Commission has been on practices at the lowest stages of the hierarchy, including a divisive and unnecessary emphasis on legislating against landfill, which is Britain's 'best practicable environmental option'. A deeper problem is that the waste hierarchy is embedded in the British way, owing little or nothing to EU membership.

Chapter 4 explores water quality, with particular reference to inland and coastal surface waters. Britain is leaving the regime, and above all the Water Framework Directive, nowhere near compliant with the EU objective of all water bodies to be of 'good status' by 2015 (with 'good' being defined as the next level down from pristine, in terms of a number of parameters that must all be met). Less than 40 per cent of Britain's rivers and estuaries currently comply, but all Member States are in a similar position.[29] The difficulty with the 'EU good' parameter in this field is that it is unrealistically rigid. In contrast, the 'British good' yardstick is more incremental and pragmatic. Thus, the pre-Water Framework Directive domestic target was to reduce the number of poor-quality rivers, whilst improving the percentage that is good, with good being defined historically as 'wholesome'. A very high proportion of watercourses (95%) satisfied the 'British good' objective in 2008 – the year before the shift to the EU version and the concomitant downgrading of good waters.

---

[28] European Environment Agency, *Municipal Waste Management Across European Countries* (May 2017) Figure 3.1, available at https://www.eea.europa.eu/themes/waste/municipal-waste/municipal-waste-management-across-european-countries.

[29] N Voulvoulis et al, 'EU Water Framework Directive: From Great Expectations to Problems of Implementation' (2017) 575 *Science of the Total Environment* 358.

Furthermore, domestic regulatory law standards co-exist alongside the common law riparian entitlement to 'purity' (again pragmatically defined), the enforcement of which is assisted by a specialist litigation union dating back to the late 1940s, called the Anglers Cooperative Association (now Fish Legal).[30]

Chapter 5 addresses air quality. As Britain leaves the EU, the European Commission is proceeding against the Government for alleged breach of the Ambient Air Quality Directive 2008, in respect of roadside concentrations of nitrogen dioxide in a number of towns and cities in England and Wales. Loss of the Commission's jurisdiction in this and other fields is seen by some as a risk, which justifies section 16 of the European Union (Withdrawal) Act 2018 (providing that the Government must put before Parliament a Bill creating a public authority charged with the task of taking proportionate enforcement action in circumstances where it 'considers that a Minister for the Crown is not complying with environmental law'). Yet the Commission's recent enforcement action in the air pollution sphere is not, I argue, a model of proportionate enforcement. The Commission has been tardy in this field, for its proceedings have been pre-empted by a series of domestic judicial review applications against the Government aimed at enforcing limit values under the Directive, brought by London-based charity Client Earth. There is nothing in the British way against the principle of health-based ambient air quality standards underpinning the Directive, and thus no question of the current limit values that take domestic effect as retained law being diluted post-Brexit. The question, rather, is whether there is a significant-enough gap in environmental governance needing to be filled by a new domestic watchdog, given the impressive way in which domestic courts and civil society have combined to put pressure on the executive here.

Chapter 6 considers nature conservation. The Habitats Directive 1992 aims to protect habitats of 'Community significance' in what is the world's largest wildlife conservation network, called Natura 2000. Britain is widely considered a reluctant participant in this regime, but this is because the idea of a habitat of 'Community interest' does not

---

[30] See *Pride of Derby v British Celanese* [1953] 2 WLR 58 (including Lord Denning's remarks about private law being the more effective path of rivers pollution prevention relative to regulation). The litigation union that funded this claim is now known as Fish Legal. See further Roger Scruton, who considers this case exemplary of the 'great advantages of our bottom up legal system' (R Scruton, *Where We Are: The State of Britain Now* (Bloomsbury 2017) 125).

easily fit within a British way that emphasises national and sub-national yardsticks of significance, originating in the National Parks and Access to the Countryside Act 1949. Furthermore, the Community regime inspires little confidence because of the low expectations of compliance and the even lower levels of performance in practice. In particular, the EU has a target of one-third of regulated habitats being in favourable or unfavourable but improving condition by 2020 – a target set in relation to the UN Biodiversity Convention 1992, of which the EU is a contracting party. But compliance with this 'modest' objective is remote, because only a one-sixth of sites are currently up to standard. By contrast, Britain and Northern Ireland (which is independently a contracting party to the Biodiversity Convention) has a target of 95% good/improving condition, applicable to 7,000 sites of special scientific interest (SSSIs) (or areas of special scientific interest (ASSIs) in Northern Ireland). The current practice is an encouraging 94%. This success is partly owing to 'unofficial' habitat conservation, through estates in land, many trust-based, alongside specific and generalised regulatory land use controls.

In conclusion (chapter 7), one of the main outcomes of this study of the British way in the context of Brexit is, I hope, to have offered an alternative to the narrative that Britain was the 'Dirty Man of Europe' until its ways were mended under the discipline of the EU. One way of interpreting the 'Dirty Man' rhetoric which my book questions is empirical. As a claim that Britain's environment and environmental policy and law was relatively poor environmentally (including in environmental policy and law terms), it does not withstand scrutiny. What *is* supportable is an interpretation which focuses on the shaming element of the rhetoric, as a valuable antidote to complacency. On this interpretation the message is 'could *always* do better', and that is integral to the British way's unending pragmatism.

Another conclusion concerns what it means within the British way to 'do better'. The United Kingdom Environmental Law Association (UKELA), in association with Kings College London, considered this issue a short time before the idea of the Remain/Leave referendum had taken shape, in a comprehensive review of the state of national environmental law (focusing on legislation).[31] The criteria for measuring

---

[31] United Kingdom Environmental Law Association and King's College London, *The State of UK Environmental Legislation in 2011: An Interim Report* (UKELA and King's College London 2011).

efficacy employed in the UKELA review are 'clarity', 'coherence' and 'integration'.[32] I adopt similar criteria of *simplicity* and *rationality* (the latter bringing together 'coherence' and 'integration'). I also add two further criteria tailored to Brexit. These are *accountability* and *autonomy*. Given a choice between a British way independent of the EU environmental acquis on the one hand, and one tied to it on the other, my core conclusion is that each of these criteria support independence.

---

[32] Ibid 16–17.

2

The British Way of
Environmental Protection

THIS CHAPTER ELABORATES on the British way of environmental protection as a paradigm within which to understand Brexit as a positive development. The term 'British way' emerged in the Ashby Report, the first of four reports commissioned by the Secretary of State for the Environment in preparation for the Stockholm Conference.[1] It appeared as a headline: 'The British Way: Each Case on its Merits.'[2] The things to explore in this chapter concern, first, the idea of an approach to environmental protection that is 'British', understood both as nationally specific and universal (all nations or nation-like groupings have their *own* way of environmental protection); second, the notion of a 'way' as an interplay of law and culture which helps society perform vital jobs; and, third, a 'British way' characterised by pragmatism – an emphasis on 'each case on its merits'.

Complexity is a defining feature of the British way, according to the Ashby Report. It comprises a 'complex web of legal and administrative measures which have been built up over the years'.[3] Donald Denman's foreword to the first environmental law 'textbook', by Alistair Bigham, made a similar point:

> Those who would comprehend the law as it stands today for the protection of the environment will find an extensive web, a ready woven gossamer of statutory texts and case law stretching back into the past …[4]

The British way is complex because of its rich history, and because it unfolds within a jurisdiction in which common law protection of the

---

[1] E Ashby et al, *Pollution: Nuisance or Nemesis* (HMSO 1972).
[2] ibid 58.
[3] ibid.
[4] DR Denman, 'Foreword' in A Bigham, *The Law Relating to the Environment* (Oyez 1972) v.

environment and statutory protection exist 'side by side' at any given moment.[5] Intriguingly, the Ashby Report suggested that common law is 'in some ways a more powerful weapon than statute law',[6] which is something the following analysis looks at closely.

The attraction of the British way theme in relation to Britain's withdrawal from the EU is that it is both a description of approaches to environmental protection and a justification for them; it is empirical and normative, in the circular way that Karl Llewellyn theorised 'law-ways' in his law jobs theory. Law works the way it works (for Llewellyn) because it *works*! In the context of Brexit, this invites serious reflection on the extent to which Britain entered the Community believing it had the know-how, the tools, the legal craft-skills necessary to protect the environment without the help of a new, supranational jurisdiction.

This chapter sets out the British way paradigm in six sections. It begins with a regulatory law perspective, with reference to David Vogel's influential analysis of regulatory 'style', before moving on to the common law aspect (including Scots law's common law-civilian law hybrid) – paying particular regard to property and tort. Attention is then given to the suggestion sometimes made by advocates of a soft Brexit that Britain entered the Community a laggard nation in respect of domestic policy and law. This is at the heart of the Remain campaign argument that Britain has improved in the company of progressive nations and a progressive EU (and ipso facto has much to lose from 'taking back control'). Attention is next given to the British way on the international stage. The chapter ends with an overview of the anticipated objections to a British way-driven Brexit, including the possibility that the British way is neither an attractive paradigm, nor one that has any real existence after decades of EU membership.

I. BRITISH WAY AND 'REGULATORY STYLE'

A helpful starting point in elaborating on the regulatory law dimension to the British way is Vogel's comparative analysis of 'styles' of regulation in Britain and the United States (US).[7] The British regulatory style,

---

[5] Ashby et al, n 1, 60.

[6] ibid.

[7] D Vogel, *National Styles of Regulation: Environmental Policy in Great Britain and the United States* (Ithaca 1986). See further D Vogel, 'The Politics of Risk Regulation in Europe and the United States' [2003] 3 *Yearbook of European Environmental Law* 1.

he suggests, is characterised by reliance on cooperation between government and business, aimed at addressing practical problems as they present themselves to protagonists, case by case.[8] By contrast, the US style is more adversarial, formal and prescriptive. Vogel writes sympathetically of British and US styles as each fit for purpose in the context of their different underlying 'national cultures'.[9]

Like the Ashby Report and the Bigham textbook already noted, Vogel places much emphasis on the historical development of regulatory law. Britain's regulatory style has taken time to 'grow'. Lessons learned are ingrained, and thus Britain (though this is not Vogel's focus) entered the European Community set in its ways. This is not to question Noga Morag-Levine's argument that Britain's early industrial regulation was 'partially ... transplanted from the continent'.[10] Undeniably, Britain's industrial pollution regulation relating to chemical works pollution was, as Morag-Levine suggests, informed by regulatory codes set out in French and German law.[11] Yet, the law and practice relating to British chemical pollution regulation nevertheless developed autonomously. Civilian law regulatory influences were domesticated within a nationally distinctive culture of public service,[12] allied to an uncodified and largely unwritten constitution reliant upon common law and convention.

Specific lessons from this early experience include the desirability of environmental goals that are realistic, in the sense of practicable, and mindful of the 'law' of unintended consequences, specifically the risk of displacing environmental problems in the course of efforts to

---

[8] Vogel, *National Styles of Regulation*, n 7, especially 21–24, and 146–92. For an 'insider' perspective, see M Holdgate, *Penguins and Mandarins: The Memoirs of Martin Holdgate* (The Memoir Club 2003) 178–80.

[9] Vogel, *National Styles of Regulation*, n 7, 23. Whilst the British approach is considered efficient in the sense that it does not spend ('waste') as much time and money on litigating contests between regulator and regulated as in the US, Vogel asserts that businesses are more profitable in the US than in Britain, which offsets the economic costs of the adversarial style (ibid 284).

[10] N Morag-Levine, 'Is the Precautionary Principle a Civil Law Instrument? Lessons from the History of the Alkali Act' (2011) 23 *Journal of Environmental Law* 1.

[11] See, eg, the influence on Lord Derby, Chair of the House of Lords Select Committee on Noxious Vapours (1862) underlying the Alkali Act 1863, of French regulatory law concerning noxious trades administered by Hygiène Publique et Salubrité, as discussed in a British Government Commissioned *Report of the Laws and Ordinances in Force in France, for the Regulation of Noxious Trades and Occupations* (HMSO 1855). Morag-Levine, n 10, 8.

[12] One thing to note is the distinctively British approach to public service. See L Fisher, 'The Enigma of Expertise' (2016) 28 *Journal of Environmental Law* 551, 553–55 (referring, inter alia, to the *failed* 'Prussian bureaucratic experiments' of Edwin Chadwick, and the success of the ideal of the generalist civil servant of Northcote Trevelyan). See further Holdgate, n 8, 185–86.

prevent them. This is illustrated by the evolution of the Alkali Acts 1863–1881. The 1863 Act required operators of chemical works to condense not less than 98 per cent of an especially noxious acid gas (hydrochloric acid gas), tasking the Alkali Inspectorate (the world's first national pollution agency) with the job of policing that rigid requirement.[13] Whilst the Inspectorate's efforts led to a substantial reduction in hydrochloric acid gas emissions, it was powerless to control other noxious gases, and it was powerless to control the waste by-products of statutory condensation (acid waste water and acidic solid waste). The Act thus was not the solution to the 'monster nuisance of all' that Parliament led the public to expect.[14] Inspectors suffered 'disrespect for administrative action which arises when political "goals" and practical implementation achievements are markedly out of line'.[15]

But lessons were learned. The Government listened to the experience of Chief Inspector Angus Smith, as well as other stakeholders (including proprietors in the vicinity of works). It proposed legislation which repurposed chemical works pollution regulation around realistic goals and flexible means of achieving them.[16] The revised Act of 1874 jettisoned the quantitative emission limit value for the singularly proscribed acid gas, replacing it with a qualitative production process standard called 'best practicable means' (bpm) applicable to a variety of acid gases, including gaseous oxides of sulphur and nitrogen.[17] Further, the bpm standard was extended (under the 1881 Act) to cover chemical

---

[13] For another relatively ambitious statute, see the Rivers Pollution Prevention Act 1876, pt III. This provided that anyone who caused poisonous, noxious or liquid pollution to flow from a manufactory committed an offence, subject to proceedings for prosecution by the local sanitary authority being approved by the Local Government Board (at Whitehall). See M Lobban, 'Tort Law, Regulation and River Pollution: The Rivers Pollution Prevention Act and its Implementation, 1876–1951' in T Arvind and J Steele (eds), *Tort Law and the Legislature: Common Law, Statute and the Dynamics of Legal Change* (Hart Publishing 2013) 329, 336.

[14] AE Dingle, 'The Monster Nuisance of All: Landowners, Alkali Manufactures and Air Pollution 1826–1864' (1982) 35 *Economic History Review* 529.

[15] Vogel, *National Styles of Regulation*, n 7, 77.

[16] The Inspectors also received a pay rise, to reflect their status as civil servant scientists of high standing within the scientific community: E Ashby and M Anderson, *Politics of Clean Air* (Oxford University Press 1981) 50.

[17] Alkali Act 1874, ss 2–4. Not all standards policed by inspectors were either statutory or process-based. An ambient water quality standard (administratively, not by statute) was set in respect of biological oxygen demand (BOD): see W Howarth, 'The History of Water Law in the Common Law Tradition' in T Tvedt, O McIntyre and T Woldetsadik (eds), *History of Water: Sovereignty and International Water Law, Vol 3* (IB Tauris & Co Ltd 2014) 66.

works emissions to water and land, in a pioneering step towards 'integrated pollution control' (IPC) a century before the term was first used. Chief Inspector Smith's successor, Alfred Fletcher, described bpm at the heart of these reforms as an 'elastic band' that tightened in response to improvements in clean technology,[18] although it also loosened in some circumstances.[19]

Nigel Haigh gives a vivid modern illustration of the elastic-band approach to bpm, with reference to flue gas desulphuration (FGD) to mitigate acid rain from power stations.[20] The Chief Inspector of the Industrial Air Pollution Inspectorate (as the Alkali Inspectorate had recently been renamed for the sake of giving a Victorian institution a modern branding, as part of a constant evolution in the domestic regulatory regime) was asked to explain why the world's first FGD technologies had been installed in two London power stations (Battersea and Fulham) between the wars, yet none had been added since. The Chief Inspector reasoned that it was a matter of each case on its merits. These early power stations were located in exceptionally densely populated areas, as well as being near beautiful metropolitan parks and Buckingham Palace. Furthermore (and harking back to the previous experience with hydrochloric acid gas condensation displacing pollution), FGD was not a panacea. It displaced pollution, resulting in acidification of the River Thames. But FGD technology had improved. As Haigh summarises:

> The Chief Inspector concluded his discussion with a scarcely veiled warning to the electricity generating industry that FGD was likely to be regarded as practicable [ie bpm] for any new fossil fuelled power station to be built in Britain – and thus required by law.[21]

This discretionary style of environmental regulation through 'warning' and other strategies aimed at 'willing' compliance is a further facet of the informality of the British way, captured in depth in Keith Hawkins' socio-legal study of river pollution inspection in the late 1970s.[22]

---

[18] See Ashby and Anderson, n 16, 40 (citing Royal Commission on Noxious Vapours 1878 PP XLIV (HMSO 1878) A Fletcher, Evidence, Q 6590).

[19] See the Inspectorate's approach to flue gas desulphurisation of power stations, n 20.

[20] N Haigh, *EEC Environmental Policy and Britain: An Essay and a Handbook* (ENDS Data Services 1984) (hereinafter '*Essay and Handbook*') 15.

[21] ibid. Ashby and Anderson point out that between 1958 and 1968, £480m was spent by Alkali Act-regulated industry on air pollution abatement technology for the purpose of bpm, including £11m by the Central Electricity Generating Board on halving emissions of particulates (Ashby and Anderson, n 16, 140).

[22] K Hawkins: *Environment and Enforcement: Regulation and the Social Definition of Pollution* (Oxford University Press 1984) 122ff ('the polluter has goodwill, co-operation

The Hawkins study is particularly interesting for its insight into the nature of the relationships – between officials, officials and wider civil society, and society and 'environment itself' – that are at the heart of the exercise of discretion within the present paradigm. Regional water authority inspectors knew their patch intimately.[23] They had an emotional attachment to the environment that sharpened their faculties of observation (the rivers were *their* rivers).[24] Yet they saw inspection as a shared effort, involving all users of rivers, notably anglers, navigators and industrial users (ie polluters) themselves. Inspectors thus sought to cooperate with members of the public (including polluters). Anglers, for example, were often the first to notice a pollution incident. This strategy tackled both instrumental (notably detection of incidents) and governance challenges (it conferred legitimacy on regulatory policing).

In America, close cooperation between inspector and inspected tends to attract the criticism of 'sweetheart regulation', and in Britain there has always been a school of thought that advocates more stringent, formalised, transparent and arm's-length inspection and enforcement strategies.[25] Occasionally, the Government has acquiesced. For example, in 1987 it replaced the Industrial Air Pollution Inspectorate with Her Majesty's Inspectorate of Pollution (HMIP), making the promise that it would take a more systematic and formal approach to enforcement based around rules (ie it would be a 'watchdog with teeth'). But many staff were relics of the Alkali Inspectorate, and for this and other reasons it proved difficult to grow confidence in a more prescriptive enforcement strategy. The established strategy of compliance over sanctioning soon re-emerged.[26]

and, most important, conformity with the law to offer'). For informality of enforcement in an alkali works setting, see C Garwood, 'Green Crusaders or Captives of Industry?: The British Alkali Inspectorate and the Ethics of Environmental Decision Making, 1864–95' (2004) 61 *Annals of Science* 99. See, in the adjacent context of waste regulation, B Lange, 'National Environmental Regulation? A Case Study of Waste Management in England and Germany' (1999) 11 *Journal of Environmental Law* 59.

[23] Hawkins, n 22, 69–70.

[24] ibid 58–61 ('field staff ... possess a considerable sense of vocation and idealism'). For a general perspective on sentiment in regulation, see B Lange, 'The Emotional Element of Regulation' (2002) 29 *Journal of Law and Society* 197.

[25] eg, Patrick McAuslan's criticisms of the 'secretive consensual' approach of inspectorates in the field of alkali and rivers pollution regulation: P McAuslan, 'The Role of Courts and other Judicial Type Bodies in Environmental Management' (1991) 3 *Journal of Environmental Law* 195, 199.

[26] A Mehta and K Hawkins, 'Integrated Pollution Control and its Impact: Perspectives from Industry' (1998) 10 *Journal of Environmental Law* 61.

Whilst (to reiterate) Vogel did not see this regulatory style leading to a 'higher level' of environmental protection than others, he considered its reliance on goodwill in addressing complex environmental challenges a virtue.[27] An area that epitomises this is pesticides and the environment.[28] Aldrin and dieldrin were by-products of nerve gas experimentation during the Second World War, that became ingredients for commercially successful organochlorine seed dressings from the late 1940s.[29] Laboratory trials by Shell (the principal producer in Britain) suggested they were 'environmentally safe' in the doses in which they were expected to be administered by farmers. In the field, however, danger was exposed when, in 1952, their extensive application in response to an epidemic of aphids poisoned hares, rabbits and birds. This was condemned by the Royal Society for the Protection of Birds, the British Trust for Ornithology and the British Field Sports Society,[30] who put pressure on farmers, pesticides suppliers and the Government to take appropriate action. Opprobrium prompted temporary restraint in pesticide usage, until an upturn in application resulted in acutely politically sensitive deaths of birds of prey.[31] In 1959, pesticides killed foxes on hunting estates – a sporting calamity.[32]

The response of the Government was to set up the Pesticides Safety Precaution Scheme, overseen by the Advisory Committee on Pesticides and Toxic Chemicals.[33] It mooted a legislative ban, but that was enough to bring to a head a 'conversation' that had been ongoing throughout the previous decade. The upshot was a voluntary moratorium on the marketing of dieldrin in spring cereal seed dressings,[34] and a wider voluntary scheme of industry self-regulation in regard to new products. The scheme placed emphasis on educating farmers as to the need for caution from

---

[27] Vogel, *National Styles of Regulation*, n 7, 25.

[28] Ibid 90–92, 93, 183–84, 274.

[29] E Russell, *War and Nature: Fighting Humans and Insects with Chemicals* (Cambridge University Press 2001). See further GS Wilson, 'Farm Safety' (1966) 23 *British Journal of Industrial Medicine* 1, 2–4; H Gay, 'Before and After Silent Spring: From Chemical Pesticides to Biological Control and Integrated Pest Management, Britain 1945–1980' (2012) 59 AMBIX 88.

[30] Whose influential president (MP John Morrison) was chairman of the Conservative Party 1922 Committee (Gay, n 29, 93).

[31] Including a 'catastrophic' effect on the peregrine falcon. See N More, 'Pesticides and Birds – A Review of the Current Situation in Great Britain 1965' (1965) 12 *Bird Study* 222, 230.

[32] Vogel, *National Styles* of Regulation, n 7, 91.

[33] Gay, n 29, 95.

[34] ibid.

a wildlife perspective. This approach appeared to work, as incidences of wildlife mortality were reduced. Vogel contrasts this informal style with the formal ban across the Atlantic in the 1960s, in response to Rachel Carson's scandalising exposé.[35]

Vogel is right to treat the response to the environmental 'troubles' of pesticides as a microcosm of the British way (or style). The experience illuminates some of the many dimensions to regulatory law and practice that are explored as my book unfolds. One is the importance of civil society – including, but not confined to, ancestral proprietors[36] – in shaping the scope and nature of legal responses to a 'given' environmental problem and, related to this, the diversity of opinion that makes it difficult to define a 'given problem' with any precision. Pesticides in Britain seemed to raise a number of discrete and somewhat contradictory problems. Some actors emphasised animal welfare concerns, with pesticides causing wild animals to die in pain and suffering.[37] Others objected to the distressing aesthetics of animal corpses spoiling scenery in areas of outstanding natural beauty – areas to which the post-war Labour Administration had given the public extended formal access (under the National Parks and Access to the Countryside Act 1949).[38] Biodiversity was another concern, yet even here there was profound complexity. Consider this passage from the Zuckerman Report:

> In approaching the problem, we were fully conscious of the fact that there is no such thing as a fixed balance of nature, and equally that every advance that has occurred in the evolution of plants and animals has meant a change in this so-called balance. Man's part in transforming the face of the earth is only the most recent contribution to a process which is as ancient as life itself.[39]

Humankind on this logic is embroiled in a circular role of shaping nature ('transforming the face of the earth') and being a part of a bigger natural history which *forms* humankind.[40]

---

[35] Vogel, *National Styles of Regulation*, n 7, 183–84. This is a reference to Carson's book *Silent Spring*, published in the US in 1962.

[36] Cf McAuslan, who distinguishes between proprietors and the general public: P McAuslan, *Ideologies of Planning Law* (Pergamon Press 1980). See further Section II of this chapter.

[37] *Toxic Chemicals in Agriculture: Risks to Wildlife. Report of the Working Party on Precautionary Measures against Toxic Chemicals used in Agriculture* (HMSO 1955) (hereinafter 'Zuckerman Report') [7].

[38] ibid [7]–[8].

[39] ibid [8].

[40] This recalls Spinoza's distinction between *natura naturata* (nature as created) and *natura naturans* (nature as creator). See C Merchant, *Autonomous Nature: Problems of Prediction and Control from Ancient Times to the Scientific Revolution* (Routledge 2015).

The 'balance of nature' conundrum is where the law jobs perspective is particularly helpful. In *The Cheyenne Way*,[41] society is portrayed as knowing the right law path to follow largely tacitly, through relationships established over generations. When disputes arise (although the authors do not touch explicitly on ecological disputes), they are resolved through 'sayings', whose wisdom the people intrinsically recognise and respect. The 'Cheyenne way' is described by Llewellyn as 'beautiful' in its functionality.[42] Beauty lies in the nearly seamlessness connection between law and culture, such that law, culture and the material environment 'play as a team' and 'sing in harmony'.[43] In an environmental setting, in an advanced industrial nation, there are going to be hard choices about 'exploitation', 'preservation' and 'conservation' of the environment, and about the relationship between humans and other living and material things or beings. The attraction of Llewellyn's perspective is that it encourages the decision maker to draw on tacit knowledge, grounded in culture, to arrive at a judgement that is respected.

I am not going to be suggesting that the British way of environmental protection is Native American in character, although there are similarities returned to below. That would be missing Llewellyn's point, which is that every well-functioning society has its own way of crafting law, including performing law-ways addressed to the ecological wellbeing of the society.[44] The theory is universal. To an extent it operates as an ideal type – it is an idea that a society may have of itself which is attractive and inspiring – but it is also empirical. It is not just a case that law jobs ought to be done; they are done – they cannot not be done, if the society is to function. Like any way on these terms, the British way doubles up both as a description of what the law does *and* as a normative account of what it ought to do.[45] However, it is important not to confuse the two. Although society needs the jobs to be done, sometimes they will not be done as they need to be, and sometimes there is dispute about 'needs'. The functionality of a way is, within the law jobs theory, under perpetual review.

---

[41] K Llewellyn and A Hoebel, *The Cheyenne Way: Conflict and Case Law in Primitive Jurisprudence* (WS Hein and Co 1941) (hereinafter '*The Cheyenne Way*').

[42] ibid 310–39. Twining expresses surprise at the emotional attachment of Llewellyn to the law's functioning. He sees it as being at the expense of a critical appreciation of the power 'structures' shaping the law: W Twining, *Karl Llewellyn and the American Legal Realist Movement*, 2nd edn (Cambridge University Press 2014) 408.

[43] *The Cheyenne Way*, n 41, 267, 269.

[44] Twining, n 42, 168–69. On ecology within the Cheyenne, see *The Cheyenne Way*, n 41, 92.

[45] *The Cheyenne Way*, n 41, 290–309. For Llewellyn the 'is' and the 'ought' are substantially intertwined. Law jobs have a 'double aspect' of ensuring survival ('the job must get

At this juncture, the point to make is that the core of the law jobs theory – and its usefulness to Brexit – is the notion of the contingent relationship between law in books and law in practice, or, as Llewellyn put it (so as to be applicable to pre-literate societies without books), the connection between law's purposes and law's effects. Llewellyn had this to say about purpose and effect: 'Without the purpose attribute, the law is unthinkable; without the effect attribute, the law cannot be said to "prevail" in a culture, to have "being" in it.'[46]

In what follows I apply this to environmental law in Britain as it leaves the EU. I am going to be looking for the 'being' EU environmental law has in Britain relative to prior law. I shall suggest that much of the protection of the environment in fields where the EU has legislated remains the product of the British way independent of the EU. To the extent that it does not, I consider the challenges arising from an already complex British way co-existing alongside and operating within an EU jurisdiction, catering for 500 million EU citizens and a large ecology supporting them.

Now it is pertinent to return to the notion that there *are* significant connections between the Cheyenne way and the British way, beyond the bare bones of a concern with law's functionality (ie beyond there being *a* way). As with the Cheyenne 'nation', Britain's laws relating to the environment unfold within an oral constitutional structure. The classic exposition of Britain's oral tradition is that of Dicey.[47] Rights and freedoms in Britain, according to Dicey, are inherent in the individual, as recognised by the courts.[48] Because they are embedded in the identity of British subjectivity, these rights 'can hardly be destroyed without a thorough revolution'.[49] The valuable practical contribution of this oral form

---

done enough to keep the group going') and betterment where possible, which Llewellyn called the 'questing aspect'. Questing is the pursuit of more adequate ways of doing the job, economically, socially, aesthetically and in terms of values such as justice (including 'justice, finer justice, ideal justice') (ibid 292).

[46] *The Cheyenne Way*, n 41, 20.

[47] AV Dicey, *Introduction to the Study of the Law of the Constitution*, 8th edn (Macmillan 1915).

[48] ibid 121. Dicey writes, 'with us [the British], the rules which in foreign countries form part of a constitutional code, are not the source but the consequence of the rights of individuals, as defined and enforced by the courts ..., thus the constitution is the result of the ordinary law of the land'. On recent judicial applications of Dicey's notion of fundamental common law rights and freedoms, see cases beginning with *R v Secretary of State for the Home Department, ex parte Pierson* [1998] AC 539 and including *R (Unison) v Lord Chancellor* [2017] UKSC 51.

[49] Dicey, n 47, 120.

in Britain is considered by Dicey, and also by opponents who take a more political view of the constitution,[50] to lie in its stability *and* flexibility. I consider stability and flexibility to be shared attributes of Cheyenne and British groupings.

This has prompted some stark contrasts between flexible and rigid ways. Consider in this respect the comments of Eric Ashby, in a book co-authored with Mary Anderson on air pollution regulation:[51]

> There is ... a basic difference between the environmental policies of Britain and the European Community. It is a difference, we think, of jurisprudence. In Britain we are accustomed to a legal system based on the common law, which grows by the gradual accretion of precedents. Other nations in the Community have a different legal system which grows by successive decrees from above. There is a Cartesian elegance about the tidy, comprehensive legislation which aims to harmonise policies for clean air and water over the length and breadth of Europe. British legislation must appear to our fellow Europeans to be pragmatic, piecemeal, ad hoc, the product of expedience not principle: a policy to be described as a non policy.[52]

This may seem a 'pantomime' characterisation, and to the extent that it is, it is echoed by Michael Carpentier, writing from a European Commission perspective:

> [W]e certainly recognise the long experience of Britain in environmental matters ... But ... incredible as it may seem, the rest of Europe do not necessarily agree on the axioms that are close to the heart of British experts and officials. For example the 'continentals' tend to believe more in standards defined on the basis of best technical means and applied through mandatory instruments. They mistrust systems based on goodwill and voluntary compliance ... they have serious doubts about the absorptive capacity of the environment.[53]

---

[50] For a critique of Dicey that nonetheless recognises the connection between stability and flexibility, see JAG Griffiths, 'The Political Constitution' (1979) 42 *Modern Law Review* 1. See too M Loughlin, *The Idea of Public Law* (Oxford University Press 2003) 30: 'the subject of public law cannot be grasped without having regard to a myriad of informal practices concerning the manner in which the activity of governing is conducted'.

[51] Ashby and Anderson, n 16.

[52] ibid 152–53.

[53] M Carpentier, *The European Community's Environmental Programme to Date* (National Council for Social Serive 1977) 7. Carpentier was writing as Director of the European Commission's Environment and Consumer Protection Service). Ruth Levitt, citing this statement, considered it 'misleadingly exaggerated' (R Levitt, *Implementing Public Policy* (Croom Helm 1980) 94). In her view, 'the differences are a matter of nuance and interpretation' (ibid). Nonetheless, she acknowledges that relations between Britain and the Commission in this field were 'acrimonious', and considers that Britain '*earned*'[my emphasis] its reputation for being 'difficult and uncooperative' (ibid 93).

In each of these passages emphasis is being placed on Britain as different from the 'rest of Europe' (Carpentier) and 'fellow Europeans' (Ashby). The book explores this dichotomy more closely in particular case study settings.

II. PROPERTY IN LAND AND THE BRITISH WAY

In the reference to the 'common law' in section I, Ashby is thinking of a *regulatory* common law, denoting a method of standard setting based on precedent: that is, regulatory standards in force at a given time are proven to work (those that do not having been discarded). Regulatory law is 'contained' in the experience of regulation, which teaches that environmental protection can go a long way on 'goodwill' and 'voluntarism' (as opposed, say, to compulsion).[54] Yet common law has a specific meaning to lawyers, denoting law arising from adjudication, about which Ashby, Vogel and others working within a political science discipline have less to say. My analysis is concerned with each of these meanings of the common law, and, crucially, the inter-relationship between the two. It is in the combination of a common law of regulation and a common law (or hybrid common law and civilian law in Scotland) of adjudication that Britain's way of environmental protection is most distinctive and, I argue, compelling.

An area of common law of particular relevance to the environment concerns property in land. Property occupies an ambivalent place in environmental law scholarship, as some see it in pejorative terms of exclusivity and exploitation for private gain.[55] But exclusivity here can work in practice to the benefit of the environment, where, say, it is pollution that is excluded. During the British Industrial Revolution, property *in land* played its part in giving plaintiffs standing to sue industrial polluters in

---

[54] Cf Carpentier, above n 53.

[55] eg M Horwitz, *Transformations in American Law, 1780–1860* (Harvard University Press 1977); K Bosselmann, 'Environmental and Human Rights in an Ethical Context' in L Kotze and A Grear (eds), *Research Handbook on Human Rights and the Environment* (Edward Elgar 2015); B Weston and D Bollier, *Green Governance: Economics, Human Rights and the Law of the Commons* (Cambridge University Press 2013). Cf B France-Hudson, 'Surprisingly Social: Private Property and Environmental Management' (2017) 30 *Journal of Environmental Law* 101. For a distinction between private property and stewardship, see W Lucy, 'Replacing Private Property: The Case for Stewardship' (1996) 55 *Cambridge Law Journal* 566; and E Barritt, 'Conceptualising Stewardship in Environmental Law' (2014) 26 *Journal of Environmental Law* 1.

private nuisance, and the financial means to execute standing.[56] Picking up on land tenure as an aspect of particular relevance to environmental law, a distinctive feature of tenure in Britain is the importance of private trust or (in Scotland) trust-like devices.

One high-profile private trust of considerable practical importance is the members-owned charity called the National Trust for Places of Historic Interest and Natural Beauty (National Trust),[57] with a membership today of over 5 million.[58] It has custody of 600,000 acres of 'heritage land' (1 per cent of the territory of Great Britain and Northern Ireland). Its early leaders included GM Trevelyan, whose popular works of social history tell of the struggle to protect the countryside and its natural beauty from the threats of industrialisation and commercialisation.[59] Trevelyan supported the gift of his family seat (Wallington Hall) to the Trust,[60] envisaging that other landed families who wanted to secure the future of 'their' estates in the face of rural economic hardship and progressive (redistributive) taxation would follow suit. Yet whilst the National Trust has subsequently grown considerably, so have the fortunes of the landed families who created it. Contrary to Trevelyan's expectations, rural land values increased, meaning that throughout the post-war era, and into the twenty first century, family seats have been able to survive independently of the National Trust.[61]

What is extraordinary is the extent to which politicians across the political spectrum have been sympathetic to the positive environmental

---

[56] I draw here on the discussion in B Pontin, 'The Common Law Clean up of the "Workshop of the World": More Realism about Nuisance Law's Historic Achievements' (2013) 40 *Journal of Law and Society* 173. This offers a revision of the earlier position set out by J Brenner, 'Nuisance Law and the Industrial Revolution' (1974) 3 *Journal of Legal Studies* 403 and JPS McLaren, 'Nuisance Law and the Industrial Revolution – Some Lessons from Social History' (1983) 3 *Oxford Journal of Legal Studies* 155. On the elite politics of nineteenth-century nuisance litigation, see B Pontin, 'Nuisance Law and the Industrial Revolution: A Reinterpretation of Doctrine and Institutional Competence' (2012) 75 *Modern Law Review* 1010.

[57] National Trust Act 1907, incorporating the National Trust for Places of Historic Interest and Natural Beauty. Some National Trust land is held under this Act on an 'inalienable' basis.

[58] 'National Trust memberships hit new high of five million', BBC News, 23 September 2017, available at http://www.bbc.co.uk/news/uk-41361095. See further National Trust, *Annual Report 2016–2017* (National Trust 2017), available at https://www.nationaltrust.org.uk/documents/annual-report-201617.pdf.

[59] GM Trevelyan, *Illustrated English Social History*, vol 4 (Longman 1949). For an outstanding commentary on Trevelyan's brand of rural environmentalism, see D Cannadine, *GM Trevelyan: A Man in History* (Yale University Press 1992).

[60] Cannadine, *GM Trevelyan*, n 59 256.

[61] D Cannadine, *The Decline and Fall of the British Aristocracy* (Vintage 1999) 651–52.

function played by hereditary landlords, notwithstanding that this runs counter to any obvious interpretation of 'fair shares' in landownership and social justice more broadly. The Labour Government of Clement Attlee (1945–50) saw gentry and aristocrats as a 'guild' of stewards who maintained the beauty of the countryside and dignified crafts of village life carried on in pastoral settings.[62] Statutory national parks created under the Act of 1949 were not 'national' in the ownership sense of industries in the fields of coal, rail, shipping (ie nationally owned). They remained in private hands, subject to public claims of access to the environmental 'services' they provided.[63] So did areas of outstanding natural beauty. This is not something that Kevin Cahill addresses in his exposé of inequitable concentration of ownership in the hands of aristocrats (as well as the Forestry Commission and the Crown).[64]

Concentration of landownership is taken furthest in Scotland, where residually feudal tenure currently accounts for ownership of half the countryside vesting in the hands of 432 proprietors.[65] But this should not detract from a similar pattern in England and Wales, where roughly one-third of the land is held in private trusts for the benefit of the leaders of 'old' landed families. Whilst that is down from about two-thirds in the nineteenth century – owing largely to tenant farmer acquisitions between the wars – it is still a large portion, dwarfing that of the National Trust.[66] One of the most extensive current English settled landholdings is the Alnwick estate in Northumberland, belonging to the Percy family. The family arrived with William the Conqueror in the eleventh century, and for the last 500 years its heads have enjoyed custody of an estate which today covers about 130,000 acres (down from 180,000 acres in Victorian

---

[62] See, eg, the nostalgic attitude to rural crafts and the British countryside of Nye Bevan, *In Place of Fear* (Simon & Schuster 1952) 34–36. Bevan boasted of his intimate knowledge of the South Wales landscape: see HC Deb 8 December 1953, vol 521, col 1903.

[63] See A Tansley, 'Nature Reserves and Nature Conservation' (1944) 13 *Journal of Ecology* 4; and RB Verney et al, *Natural Resources: Sinews for Survival* (HMSO 1972) [150]. Cf the unimplemented recommendations of the Ramsay Committee, discussed in ch 6 of this book.

[64] K Cahill, *Who Owns Britain and Ireland: The Hidden Facts Behind Landownership in the UK and Ireland* (Canongate 2001). See below, n 109 and associated text.

[65] Land Reform and Review Group, *The Land of Scotland and the Common Good* (Land Reform Review Group 2014) 160 (this is a little less concentrated than in Victorian times, when 1,380 families owned 90% of Scotland's territory).

[66] On landed society in Victorian times, including patterns of ownership, see FML Thompson, *English Landed Society in the Nineteenth Century* (Routledge 1971). On inter-war sales, see Cannadine, n 61, ch 14.

times). That is one-tenth of England's fifth-largest county. The estate seems well cared for environmentally.[67]

Being private is not a criticism in law jobs terms if the effect is that the environment is well protected *and* the wider public benefits as a consequence. That is the justification elite proprietors have always offered for things being this way, and it is a justification that impressed Max Nicholson, who captures particularly well the centre-left tolerance of the landed elite, in his romantic description of patrician landownership as the 'antithesis of the distorted and artificial approach of classical economics'.[68]

> By setting themselves against the divorce of land from nature and society and its subjection to the real estate market economy British landowners have rendered a ... notable service ... Their conservatism has proved of great value in maintaining almost intact far into the twentieth century the landscape inheritance derived from the seventeenth and eighteenth, complete with trees, hedgerows, field patterns, wild or feral rivers, pools and marshy places.[69]

This is an early variation on Ben France-Hudson's recent analysis of property law working in 'surprisingly social' ways (with reference to New Zealand).[70] What Nicholson is describing is similar to France-Hudson's 'enduring counter-tradition', set against an economically liberal conception of property.

This is not to say that there is not also room for a *public* trust doctrine. A version of this exists in relation to the public right of navigation and fishing in the sea, including rights to access the sea from the foreshore. In the *Newhaven* case,[71] the Supreme Court considered Best J's dissenting judgment in *Blundell v Catterall*,[72] namely, that as

---

[67] Northumberland Estates, 'Conservation' (at http://www.northumberlandestates. co.uk/the-estate/conservation/). See further ch 5. On the more general role of 'living' relationships between people and property in land onto which my analysis opens, see S Blandy, S Bright and S Nield, 'The Dynamics of Enduring Relationships of Property in Land' (2018) 81 *Modern Law Review* 85.

[68] M Nicholson, *The Environmental Revolution: A Guide for the New Masters of the Earth* (Hodder and Stoughton 1970) 149. Nicholson was a senior civil servant in the Atlee Administration 1945–1950, playing an influential role in the drafting of the National Parks and Access to the Countryside Act 1949. See P Ayers, *Shaping Ecology: The Life of Arthur Tansley* (Wiley-Blackwell 2012) 159–60. He was Director General of Nature Conservancy 1952–66.

[69] Nicholson, *The Environmental Revolution*, n 68.

[70] France-Hudson, n 55.

[71] R *(on the application of Newhaven Port and Properties Ltd) v East Sussex County Council* [2015] UKSC 7.

[72] *Blundell v Catterall* (1821) 106 ER 1190.

land is held by the monarch for the benefit of all subjects, any private right to use and enjoy lacks exclusivity (it is 'subject to public trust'). The Supreme Court restated the majority opinion in *Blundell*, that the doctrine was not part of domestic common law. Yet common law is adaptable, and there is an argument (put by Emily Shirley and Marc Willers) that Best J's approach will find new support as Britain looks for creative national legal forms outside the EU.[73] This can draw succour from Lord Carnwath's opinion in *Newhaven*, that the doctrine of public trust 'might yet develop'.[74]

III. THE BRITISH WAY ON THE LEADER-LAGGARD SPECTRUM

The British way, then, is intensely complex, and accurately described by Denman as richly textured fabric built up over many generations.[75] However, that makes it hard to compare with environmental law in codified jurisdictions, or, rather, hard to compare sympathetically. This is illustrated by Rudi Wurzel's comparison of British, German and EU air and water pollution regulation.[76] Britain and Germany are portrayed as at opposite ends of the environmental leader-laggard spectrum, but which is which? Wurzel sees Germany as *the* 'environmental leader state', because it had more proposals for environmental legislation in the early 1970s than any of its fellow Member States. Between 1973 and 1977 Germany notified to the European Commission 28 draft national environmental legislative measures. Britain notified two.[77]

The leader-laggard spectrum is quite useful as an ideal-type analytical device, but there are difficulties with Wurzel's application of it to draft enactments. One is that it is skewed in favour of Germany, and the broader civilian law tradition in which it fits, as not all law in a common law tradition starts with a legislative proposal that ends with an enactment. Significant parts of it are 'unwritten'. Second, written parts of environmental law in Britain are often older and more established than in

---

[73] M Willers and E Shirley, 'The Public Trust Doctrine's Role in Post Brexit Britain', *Garden Court Chambers Working Paper* (31 March 2017), available at www.gardencourt-chambers.co.uk/the-public-trust-doctrines-role-in-post-brexit-britain/.

[74] *Newhaven*, n 71, [130].

[75] Denman, n 4.

[76] R Wurzel, *Environmental Policy-Making in Britain, Germany and the European Union* (Manchester University Press 2006) 77.

[77] ibid 76–77, citing Council of European Experts, *Umveltgutachten 1978* (Bundestags, Drukstache 8/1938).

Europe's newer jurisdictions (exemplified by West Germany in Wurzel's analysis), and thus do not register on a scale of *recent* draft legislation.[78] Third, the idea that anything can be read into the quantity (rather than quality) of draft or enacted measures is improbable. One of Britain's two proposals (the Protection of Environment Bill 1973, which was enacted as the Control of Pollution Act 1974) was an omnibus measure that built on legislation dating back to Victorian times in regard to waste, water and air pollution, whilst adding to this new regulatory law in the field of noise.

My characterisation of the British way thus challenges the impression some have of it as laggardly. That Britain started out as a reticent *partner* in the development of an acquis communitaire regarding the environment is undeniable. But that was because it could not see the point of such development, and was anxious that the British way would be weakened. The development of nascent EU environmental law appeared to Baroness Emmet, examining witnesses to a Select Committee on Environmental Problems and the EC Treaty, 'extremely dangerous' and potentially 'disastrous'.[79] Emmet was unpersuaded of the problem to which Community competence was a solution. What could be gained by the British way's working alongside (or being subsumed within) a Community way, in which directives set objectives that are obligatory, with Member States having some discretion as to their execution, subject to Community oversight?

This was the concern underpinning Lord Diplock's questioning of Nigel Haigh and other witnesses representing the Committee for Environmental Conservation (CoEnCo),[80] an early green alliance umbrella group: 'Have you considered to what extent you wish to hand over environmental control to the institutions of the Community and the extent to which it is dealt with nationally?'[81] Nigel Haigh (speaking on behalf of the Institute of European Environmental Policy) answered

---

[78] Haigh makes the important observation that 'Novelty, clarity and a measure of detail are the characteristics of national legislation that will render it likely to influence the Community, and the style of British legislation largely disqualifies it'. (*Essay and Handbook*, n 20, 303). See too A Jordan, *The Europeanization of British Environmental Policy: A Departmental Perspective* (Palgrave Macmillan 2002) 31: 'when the EU began to take an interest in the environment Britain had relatively little new policy to submit to the Commission … because it had effectively already legislated'.

[79] House of Lords Select Committee on the European Communities, *Environmental Problems and the Treaty of Rome*, Session 1979–1980, HL 68 (HMSO 1980).

[80] This was founded in 1969 and continued into the early 1980s, when it was subsumed within Wildlife Link (see now at https://www.wcl.org.uk/).

[81] House of Lords Select Committee, n 79, q16.

that some areas were clearly better suited to Community-wide regulation, with others better suited to national level regulation. In the middle is a grey area. An example was given of wild birds regulation:

> In many ways you could say that what you do with birds is a matter for each member state, but the recent community action was taken because it was perfectly well understood that in no way would Italy and France have legislated to protect migratory birds.[82]

This is fascinating. Is this (i) a clear case for national control ('what you do with birds is a matter for each Member State');[83] (ii) a clear case for Community action ('action was taken' because it was perfectly clear that the main 'offenders' would not take action themselves); or (iii) a grey area?[84]

IV. THE BRITISH WAY AND INTERNATIONAL ENVIRONMENTAL LAW

One of the main objections to Community competence in the evidence session noted in section III was from peers who were not persuaded that it had anything practical to add to the competences of UN and regional intergovernmental bodies. Picking up on the question posed by Lord Diplock, the Earl of Cranbrook asked why it was desirable to protect migratory birds through the European Community, rather than (or in addition to) under the Convention on the Conservation of Migratory Species of Wild Animals 1979 (Bonn Convention).[85] Haigh's response was that an international convention typically has no domestic force in Britain unless the legislature has incorporated it into domestic law – a 'limitation' that does not apply to Community legislation.

Liz Fisher makes a timely point that 'for good or for ill, political and legal imagination is the product of legal communities that cluster into nation states'.[86] Non-governmental green organisations, perhaps

---

[82] ibid.

[83] See W Wils, 'Subsidiarity and EU Environmental Policy: Taking People's Concern Seriously' (1994) 6 *Journal of Environmental Law* 85, 87 ('many of the birds protected under the Birds Directive are not migratory').

[84] See n 90 and associated text.

[85] ibid Q17. Convention on the Conservation of Migratory Species of Wild Animals (1989) 19 ILM 15.

[86] E Fisher, *Environmental Law: A Very Short Introduction* (Oxford University Press 2017) 66.

epitomised in the early history of their development by the CoEnCo, can see nation states as potential obstacles to environmental protection. But they are not obstacles that are easily overcome. Nation states (as Fisher puts it pithily) 'structure the world': 'they are the communities around which political and legal responses to environmental problems coalesce'.[87] They 'contain' legal cultures that overlap with political ones, through constitutions that legitimate law institutions domestically and on the international stage.

Bringing this back to birds, that is why the House of Lords Select Committee and its witnesses from the CoEnCo disagreed over the merits of Community competence. For British peers, the sovereignty of Italy and France in respect of migratory birds was of the utmost significance. It was not for some supranational body to outlaw this culturally ingrained, rural practice. The better course of action was for nations that objected to put this on the agenda of intergovernmental diplomacy, leading to an international agreement that could be signed, and ratified, by the countries concerned. Italy and Spain signed the Bonn Convention.

In a later work, Haigh returns to birds, as follows:

> Some argue that there is no such thing as a European public opinion [on habitats and wildlife matters], given that opinion is grounded in national traditions, language and history ... The point is well made by the southern European who reluctantly admitted that many of his fellow countrymen thought it unacceptable to eat protected wild birds, unlike outraged northerners who, as he said, poisoned them with pesticides instead.[88]

The tabloid paper, *Daily Express*, has covered this issue under the nationalistic headline, 'British robins slaughtered in Southern Europe'.[89] The author of that piece is not, however, advocating enforcement of EU law. He is advocating diplomatic pressure.

Unsurprisingly, then, the British way on an international stage shares many of the characteristics it has domestically. It values cooperation, discretion, exhortation and goodwill. The case studies explored in this book provide an opportunity to look closely at the merits of the House of Lords Select Committee's stance. Was it right to see no 'need' for EU

---

[87] ibid 67.

[88] N Haigh, *EU Environmental Policy: Its Journey to the Centre Stage* (Routledge 2016) 9.

[89] S Winter, 'Skinned and Ready to Eat: British Robins Among 25m Bird Slaughtered in Southern Europe', *Daily Express*, 22 August 2015. The basis is Birdlife International, *The Killing* (Birdlife International 2015). It reports (at 9) that 5.6m birds are illegally killed annually in Italy alone.

competence, given national sovereignty and international law? Maria Lee draws on political science literature to posit three needs (or reasons) for EU regulation, all of which concern 'spillovers' from the nation state: physical, economic and psychic.[90] The birds scenario seems to have elements of all three, in that many (but not all)[91] of the regulated species are migratory (a 'physical spillover'); they are a raw material for food in some countries (an 'economic spillover'); and some find their killing for food abhorrent (a 'psychic spillover'). But how significant a spillover in these respects are they? There are two ways in which they may not justify EU competence: first, where they are too small in all three respects to legitimately engage the EU jurisdiction; second, where they are too large to be confined to a jurisdiction limited to the EU-28.

Leading on from this is the place of the EU within a wider international order. Much of the EU literature assumes that the EU is a significant influence on the international stage, and that Britain's international voice is more powerful within the EU as a consequence. During the Review of Competences, it was pointed out by Nigel Haigh and other witnesses that there was much 'goodwill' surrounding 'Team EU' internationally, particularly in the climate sphere.[92] That was true at the time. However, it seems that the international community is increasingly wise to the difficulties the EU has in the climate field, with the totality of the Member States of the EU being a microcosm of the 'leaders' and 'laggards' the world over. That is to say it is jurisdiction covering countries whose greenhouse gas emissions are rising and those whose emissions are falling. Britain arguably has a higher standing individually than the EU as a whole, by virtue of the ambitious Climate Change Act 2008 and, crucially, the fact that Britain is on track to comply with it. For example, Britain's national carbon budget is for greenhouse gas emission reductions of 57 per cent by 2030, against a baseline of 1990. The current reduction is 40 per cent, equating to Britain's carbon footprint in 1890. This is compared to the EU's modest current reduction of 23 per cent, which is some way off the relatively modest target for 2030 (40% reduction).

Digging deeper, this links with the issue of what Boryana Gotsova calls the 'public spats' involving the EU and its Member States

---

[90] M Lee, *EU Environmental Law: Challenges, Change and Decision Making* (Hart Publishing 2005) 10. See further Wils, n 83, 88ff.

[91] See ibid 87.

[92] Her Majesty's Government, *Review of the Balance of Competences between the United Kingdom and European Union: Environment and Climate Change* (Crown Copyright 2014) 45.

in international relations in areas (ie most) where there is shared competence.[93] Unsurprisingly, the European Commission is keen to take the lead in negotiations where it has shared competence, relative to 'big' Member States like Germany and Britain. Thus it does not welcome these Member States playing an active role separate from the Commission, but it is not powerful enough to exclude them. Germany and Britain are frequently in dispute with the Commission about the amount of time the Member State has to put its case in plenary sessions, and there are also spats about use of Member State rather than EU name plates. These may seem petty concerns, Gotsova writes, but they 'highlight fundamental tensions' between the Commission, Germany and Britain.[94]

Attempts to provide a united front appear not to have been successful. The Commission drafted a working practice document aiming to rationalise, and better coordinate the role of it and Member States in the conduct international negotiations.[95] However, Britain (and Germany) issued separate documents that diverged from the Commission document. Moreover, a fascinating challenge to the notion of 'goodwill' towards the European Commission in the wider international community is provided by Andrés Casteleiro.[96] He comments that the Commission tends not to submit paperwork in a timely fashion, if at all.[97] The British, he suggests, have a reputation for a more respectful attitude to international diplomacy and procedural niceties. Does it have greater goodwill internationally than the Commission? Possibly.

V. CHALLENGES TO THE BRITISH WAY ARGUMENT

So far I have alluded only briefly to the anxieties prompting many commentators to advocate a soft Brexit, if there has to be Brexit at all. Now it is necessary to elaborate on them. Two groups of concern can

---

[93] B Gotsova, 'EU's Procedure for Concluding International Treaties' (2015) 24 *European Energy and Environmental Law Review* 44. On the formal law in this field from a Brexit perspective, see R Macrory and J Newbigin, 'The United Kingdom's International Obligations After Brexit' in O Fitzgerald and E Lein (eds), *Complexity's Embrace: The International Law Implications of Brexit* (McGill-Queens University Press 2018) 243.

[94] Gotsova, n 93, 49.

[95] Council doc 15855/II ADD2, 24 October 2011.

[96] A Casteleiro, 'EU Declarations of Competences in Multilateral Agreements: A Useful Reference Based?' (2012) 17 *European Foreign Affairs Review* 491.

[97] ibid 502.

helpfully be distinguished. First, that the British way is not an attractive ideal. Second, that even if it had merit when Britain entered the Community, it no longer exists, after decades of Europeanisation, as well as erosion from within (devolution).

A. Normative Objections to the British Way

One objection is that the British way as portrayed in this chapter is seriously rose-tinted, emphasising the things that seem to be done well and ignoring weaknesses. Jeremy Bugler's book, published in 1972, called *Polluting Britain: A Report*,[98] paints a particularly dire picture that is far removed from the optimistic one Peter Walker evoked in Stockholm. Bugler's rhetorically powerful book cover is a map of Britain made up of fragments of dark particles from power station emissions (acid rain was a popular concern at that time). Landscapes scarred by slag heaps, intolerably noisy towns and cities, rivers and air poisoned with heavy metals, particles and acids in liquid or gaseous form, and declining wildlife are what Bugler notices about the 'real' environment of Britain in EEC accession year. Britain on this reasoning entered the Community deserving its 'dirty man of Europe' reputation – a rhetoric that became the cornerstone of the Green Alliance campaign for Remain during the 2016 referendum.[99]

Ashby dismisses Bugler's account as scurrilous journalism,[100] but sometimes it finds expression within the Government itself. Derek Osborn offers an 'insider's' endorsement of Bugler's message of historically poor performance in his comment that Britain was 'badly trailing' behind 'more progressive' European neighbours in the mid-1970s and 1980s.[101] An aim of this book is to look critically at the historical basis of the 'dirty man' claim, with particular reference to case studies of law and practice before and during Britain's EU membership. As indicated in section I of this chapter in relation to enforcement, there has always been a school of thought that the British way lacks urgency. Polemical journalism, and single-issue campaigning advocating 'tougher' action,

---

[98] J Bugler, *Polluting Britain: A Report* (Pelican 1972).

[99] C Rose, *The Dirty Man of Europe: The Great British Pollution Scandal* (Simon & Schuster 1991).

[100] Ashby and Anderson, n 16,125.

[101] D Osborn, 'Reflections on UK Environmental Policy, 1970-1995' (1997) 9 *Journal of Environmental Law* 1, 5.

are as much part of the British way as bpm, nuisance law and the diverse opinions of 'insiders' Eric Ashby and Derek Osborn.

A second objection is to the informality of the British way. Goodwill and trust are welcome, but as Maria Lee points out, the emphasis on discretion in a regulatory law context places a heavy burden of trust on the part of the public and of *being trusted* on the part of the regulator.[102] The EU is attractive because (most) rules are written and all citizens can request the Commission to investigate breaches:

> The special space for the enforcement of EU environmental law, through Commission action and in the national courts, will be much missed post-Brexit – not just by those who litigate, but by those who use the authority of law to shape political change.[103]

Lee gives the recent example of clean air litigation brought by Client Earth against the Government before and after the Court of Justice of the EU (CJEU) got involved, comparing the leisurely pace of the domestic legal process, and its judicial deference in the face of executive discretion, with the greater urgency once the CJEU gave its opinion of the legal issues referred to it by the Supreme Court.[104]

A third objection to the British-way ideal is the inherent limits of a *national way* of environmental protection, given that the environment (as the saying goes) knows no national boundaries. Liz Fisher remarks – in a book that is otherwise sympathetic to the nation state paradigm as a 'songline'[105] – that environmental problems are problems of places that are interconnected. The connections are economic, social and *physical*. Consider in this regard the 'continentalism' of seminal ecologist Arthur Tansley, who, whilst a patriotic champion of Britain's 'green mantle',[106] nevertheless emphasised the Continental nature of his country's ecology.

---

[102] M Lee, *Environmental Accountability After Brexit*, UCL European Institute Working Paper (UCL November 2017). A similar point was made earlier by Maurice Frankel, with respect to the opaque regulatory practices of the Alkali Inspectorate (M Frankel, *The Social Audit Pollution Handbook* (Macmillan 1978) 67–69).

[103] M Lee, 'Brexit- EU Accountability and EU Governance', 17 October 2016 (at https://blog.oup.com/2016/10/brexit-environment-eu-governance/).

[104] Ibid 5. This is not to suggest that Lee considers EU air pollution law robust, or the Commission's response to breaches diligent. See M Lee, Evidence, Environmental Audit Committee, *EU and UK Environmental Policy*, Third Report of Session 2015–2016, HC 537. See further ch 5 of this book.

[105] Fisher, n 86, 66 ('The significance of nation states is a songline that forges meaning – a set of legal practices that frame legal understanding of what is possible').

[106] A Tansley, *Britain's Green Mantle*, 2nd edn (Allen & Unwin 1968). See ch 6 of this book.

Britain is demarcated from the Continent by a 'very shallow layer of water which ... isolates the British Isles, thinning to a mere film, as it were ... between south eastern England and the opposite coasts of north eastern France, Belgium, Holland, Germany, Denmark'.[107] He continued by suggesting that 'In every sense, then, the British Isles are "continental islands" very recently separated from the continent.'[108]

A fourth objection to the ideal is that it does not reflect modern values. Aristocrats protecting foxes from pesticides when not hunting them ritualistically is an old-fashioned way of conserving nature.[109] Dukes holding estates of six-figure acreages based on medieval title may mean that land is protected from market forces, but it is a closed and deeply anachronistic tenure, so the objection goes. The EU is more economically and politically liberal. This important concern can be framed in law jobs terms in relation to law's 'questing' aspect.[110]

B. Existential Objections

The foregoing remarks presuppose that there is still a British way, but is there? National and EU laws have, as Jordan points out, 'co-evolved',[111] each altering the other such that there is no going back. Britain's environmental laws since entry have become more formalised – some things that were left to administrative discretion are now formalised in secondary legislation. Equally, EU environmental law has been shaped in the British image, with greater emphasis on ambient quality standards, on broad qualitative criteria such as 'good status' for rivers, and more generally the EU has evolved in an organic fashion, learning from experience.

An intriguing slant on this existential issue is provided by Brendan Simms, writing in a more general context. Simms strongly favours Britain's EU membership on the condition that it (the EU) learns to accept

---

[107] A Tansley, *The British Islands and their Vegetation* (Cambridge University Press 1939) 3.

[108] ibid. That is 'reflected in the flora and fauna, the great bulk of which are continental' (ibid 4).

[109] My secondhand copy of Vogel, *National Styles* of Regulation, n 7, has the handwritten marginal comment of an angry earlier reader: 'so foxes were saved from pesticides so scum could hunt them to death'.

[110] *The Cheyenne Way*, n 41, 292. On the value-expressive function of regulation, see B Morgen and K Yeung, *An Introduction to Law and Regulation: Texts and Materials* (Cambridge University Press 2007) 5–7.

[111] Jordan, *Europeanistion of British Environmental Policy*, n 78, 4. See also C Hilson, 'The Impact of Brexit on the Environment: Exploring the Dynamics of a Complex Relationship' (2018) 7 *Transnational Environmental Law* 89.

and replicate the superior functionality of the 'Westminster system'![112] To borrow from that analysis, Britain is leaving what could have been (and should have been) 'Britain's Europe'.[113] While (Simms comments) Brexiteers sometimes liken the EU to a power-grasping super-state, it is really a 'sports club', in which the most powerful players compete with one another, as others spectate. Nothing could be more British.[114] This again has a pantomime feel, but it nevertheless adds an important nuance to the criticism of the 'taking back control' narrative, which challenges not the idea of control but that Britain lacks it in the EU.

A variation on this existential point (that there is no British way as a default position once Britain leaves) concerns devolution. Britain entered the Community more centralised around the Whitehall and Westminster ways than previously, with Northern Ireland under direct rule (the Government of Ireland Act 1920 was effectively suspended between 1972 and 1998). More generally there was at most administrative devolution concerning Wales, and though Scotland tended to be legislated for separately from England and Wales within Parliament at Westminster, there was no specifically Scottish Parliament enabling the passage of Scots legislation. So much has changed, irreversibly.

VI. CONCLUSION

Returning to the law jobs theory, what the remainder of the book aims to demonstrate is that the British way really is functional in the senses outlined in this chapter, and that the noted concerns about its functionality (and existence) can be overcome. The method by which Llewellyn and Hoebel sought to elucidate the functionality of the Cheyenne way was through case studies, and it is the method used by political scientists studying British–EU relations in the environmental field. Case studies, whether they are driven by theory or are more bottom-up, will always seek to engage with a topic at the level of detail. This book aims to contribute detail to the Brexit and environment discussion in four main fields, concerning waste, water, air and nature conservation, whilst keeping sight of the overall picture of broad functionality.

---

[112] B Simms, *Britain's Europe: A Thousand Years of Conflict and Cooperation* (Allen Lane 2016) 216, 245–46.

[113] ibid 245.

[114] B Simms, 'The World After Brexit', *The New Statesman* (1 March 2017). On the connection between Britain's constitution and the norms of a 'good sport', see B Disraeli, *Lord George Bentinck: A Political Biography* (1852).

3

Waste

O N SUNDAY 9 May 1971, members of a new organisation called
Friends of the Earth marched through central London carrying
between them over a thousand non-returnable glass bottles,
which were deposited at the headquarters of Cadbury Schweppes, in
Bayswater.[1] 'Don't let them Schhh ... on Britain' was the message aimed
at one of the world's largest multinational drinks manufacturers, which
had controversially switched from supplying beverages in returnable
to non-returnable bottles. The press appreciated the humour, and the
national and international coverage the campaign received established
'the Friends' as a leading green pressure group. However, one important
person was left unmoved, at least initially – Lord Watkinson, the company chair. He dismissed the demonstration as 'a bit of nonsense'.[2] The
bottles represented 'just a quarter of an hour's production in one of
our small factories'. A letter writer in *The Times* quipped, 'The Friends
could hardly have put it better. Exactly so!'[3]

There are a number of aspects of the return to sender campaign that
make it an appropriate point of entry to the case studies concerning
Brexit and the environment. Why did a publicity seeking new environmental organisation choose the topic of waste glass as a core theme, as
opposed to, say, something more obviously 'toxic'? What did it have to
gain (or lose) from a campaign whose objectives were pro-establishment,
represented by a private system of reusable glass containers, under threat
from a brave new world of convenience food in convenient packaging?
How could it be said that Cadbury Schweppes, with their decision to

---

[1] 'Protest Group Dumps a 1000 Empties on Schweppes', *The Times* (10 May 1971);
'Bottle Campaign is no Empty Gesture of Protest', *The Times* (11 May 1971). See further
M Veldman, *Fantasy, the Bomb, and the Greening of Britain: Romantic Protest, 1945–1980*
(Cambridge University Press 1994) 224–27; D Sandbrook *State of Emergency: Britain
1970–1974* (Allen and Lane 2010) 212–13.

[2] 'Bottles Protest', *Sunday Times* (9 May 1971).

[3] 'Letters to the Editor', *The Times* (14 May 1971).

switch to disposable bottles, were harming *Britain* rather than the environment? And who said what to Lord Watkinson, that won him round to the Friends' broad position?[4] This chapter considers these and other questions as they bear on the prospects for Britain's waste as the country leaves the EU. One thing to note at the outset is the change in the position of Friends of the Earth – not on bottles, but on the benefits of EU membership from a waste perspective. From being initially sceptical about the possibility of the Common Market adding anything useful to the battle against waste,[5] the organisation has shifted towards a position of respect for a series of EU waste policies and laws formulated around the 'waste hierarchy', with prevention at the top and disposal at the bottom. The organisation values EU law highly for its opposition to landfill – for long Britain's favoured mode of disposal. Leaving the EU waste acquis, and facilitating more liberal recourse to landfill, is assessed as a 'very high risk'.[6]

The argument in this chapter is that Britain entered the EU with a strong national identity set resolutely against waste or, more positively, built on thrift and resourcefulness. That is why the organisation adopted a 'small c' conservative rhetoric of patriotism and defending the establishment in its return-to-sender campaign, and why, in Britain, this was an effective strategy in terms of engaging the public. It is also why the organisation at this time positively promoted landfill, which was and is part of Britain's identity in respect of waste. When Britain entered the EU, landfills at their best were sophisticated feats of engineering, which were more popular (or less unpopular) with locals than the alternative of incineration. Membership of the EU has meant that Britain is in a small minority on this issue, and under a supranational governance system revolving around qualified majority voting, that means a loss of control. This is all the more unsatisfactory, because of the until recent neglect within the EU of challenges higher up the waste hierarchy.

---

[4] 'During the discussions I came to the view that the Friends were doing a very sensible job. This is a general problem which includes wrapping paper, cans, bottles, the lot. Clearly, this is a matter for the Government' ('Schweppes Chief Asks for Bottles Study', *The Times* (15 November 1971)); 'Non-Returnable Bottle Inquiry Planned', *The Times* (17 November 1971).

[5] See Veldman, n 1, 247, 257; R Lamb, *Promising the Earth* (Routledge 1996) 50.

[6] C Burns, V Gravey and A Jordan, *UK Environmental Policy Post-Brexit: A Risk Assessment* (Friends of the Earth 2017) 31. Cf L Small and R Lee, *Waste Regulation Law* (Bloomsbury 2016) 1 ('What it [Brexit] may do in future is mean that a new standard on which to base UK law could be created instead of the EU Directive').

I. THE BRITISH WAY OF WASTE 1945–73

Britain's antipathy towards waste is expressed well in the natural law theorising of John Locke. In *Second Treatise on Government*, Locke asserted that 'Nothing was made by God for man to spoil or destroy'.[7] Waste was rationalised by Locke as offensive both at a metaphysical level, in denigrating the material embodiment of deity, and at the level of social justice: in a finite material world, one person's waste is another's want. In these twin senses, Locke considered waste 'offended against the common law of nature'.[8] But, as Richard Girling points out, 'waste is as necessary to life as air and water'.[9] Everything comes to an end, as it must, and thus waste cannot be wrong in absolute terms. Waste therefore cannot, as per Locke, be viewed in juristic terms as *mala in se*. Any wrongs lie in the field of its (mis)management (or *mala prohibita*).

A. Rationing: Waste as *Mala in Se*

The closest any country at any time has come to implementing Locke's categorical reasoning on waste is Britain during the post-war Attlee Administration. The Administration not only retained, but also intensified a cascade of primary and secondary legislation introduced during the Second World War, addressed to rationing, with the aim of ensuring that nothing was wasted and basic material goods were shared equally throughout the population, regardless of class or monetary wealth.[10] Rationing was a key aspect of Labour's 'fair shares' policy, which also found expression in other policy areas, particular health and industrial policy (nationalisation of core industries), as well as other aspects of environmental policy.

Rationing law is thus where the study of the evolution of British way of waste in the post-war period begins. The law was originally set out

---

[7] J Locke, *Second Treatise on Government*, ed CB Macpherson (Hacket Publishing 1980) 31.210. For an illuminating application to modern environmental issues, see S Coyle and K Morrow, *Philosophical Foundations of Environmental Law* (Hart Publishing 2004) 51.

[8] Locke, n 7.

[9] R Girling, *Rubbish! Dirt on Our Hands and the Crisis Ahead* (Transworld Publishers 2005) i (cited in E Fisher, B Lange and E Scotford, *Environmental Law: Text, Cases, and Materials* (Oxford University Press 2013) 666).

[10] Defence (General) Regulations 1939 (SI 1939/927), reg 55. For a history of rationing, touching on law and politics, see I Zweiniger Bargielowska, *Austerity in Britain: Rationing, Controls and Consumption, 1939–1955* (Oxford University Press 2000).

in the Emergency Powers (Defence) Act 1939, the General (Defence) Regulations 1939 and the Rationing Order 1939.[11] It covered all kinds of goods, including clothing, fuel, building materials and food. Paragraph 6 of the Rationing Order, concerning food, provides a helpful snapshot of the structure and content of the law:

> Except where the Minister shall otherwise authorise, rationed food may be obtained for household consumption only up to the prescribed amount, and only by means of the ration book, or leaf, or coupon, or other ration document ... lawfully used.

People buying rationed food between 1940 and 1954 had to present to the retailer a coupon to be redeemed on purchase. The coupon represented a prescribed form and 'prescribed amount', set as a maximum permissible allocation. Retailer and consumer complied with the law on pain of criminal sanction.

Rationing law had a regulatory design that is familiar to environmental lawyers. It prescribed quantitative limits on the consumption/use of natural resources (eg ½lb of bacon), rather as limit values in relation to prescribed substances are applied in the setting of environmental permits. Sometimes, the connection between rationing and environmental conditions is particularly clear, as with the decision to place potatoes 'on ration' in 1947, in response to a wet spring, dry summer and hard winter.[12] Further, regulation here operated within a complex web of legal relationships structured by private law – in this case various laws relating to property, beginning with the right to sow and harvest crops through to contracts for their sale in retail outlets.

The reported case law suggests that criminal aspects of rationing law were strictly enforced, thus constituting an intense and pervasive regulatory presence in daily life. For example, in *Keane v Adair*,[13] the appellant shopkeeper was prosecuted in a Scottish court for having 'sold ½lb of bacon to a customer without the customer using her ration book'. Ina Zweiniger Bargielowska's chapter on law enforcement bears this out. Criminal administrative enforcement of food rationing was overseen by the Ministry of Food, with policing of serious crime organised

---

[11] Rationing Order 1939 (SI 1939/1856).

[12] Potatoes (Control of Supply) Order 1947 (SI 1947/2402). See further Zweiniger Bargielowska, n 10, 83. Bread was also rationed for similar reasons, between July 1946 and 1948. Potatoes and bread were 'buffer goods' which it had never been the intention to ration. On the link between bread rationing and the scarcity of domestic supplies of as a result of Britain's post-war occupation of Germany, see B Marshall, 'German Attitudes to British Military Government' (1980) 15 *Journal of Contemporary History* 655.

[13] *Keane v Adair* [1942] SLT 16.

through 19 divisions, dealing with different types of food rationing crime at the serious end. For lesser offences, local authority officers were responsible for enforcement. Between 1945 and 1951, a total of 133,299 food-rationing prosecutions were successfully brought.[14]

Much is made in the social history literature of the health of the national diet.[15] Modest amounts of meat, dairy and confectionary produce, supplemented by non-rationed fresh produce (notably fruit and vegetables) available in season, constituted a legal national diet that was more nutritious than the 'average' diet before the war. For specific purposes of waste, however, the significance of rationing is that it entailed that very little was thrown away. In an age before waste statistics were compiled, the preventative effect of rationing is best highlighted by the lucrative market in salvaged goods. Municipal kitchen scraps had a value to local authority salvage undertakings of £2.50 per ton (more than scrap metal).[16]

On this measure, the area of rationing that exerted the strongest waste-prevention force was clothing. Rationed until 1949, garments purchased with clothing coupons were by their nature uniform. Yet they ceased to be so when their owners transformed them through person-alised addition of dye, embroidery and other innovative techniques of sartorial customisation.[17] Street fashion was paradoxically more diverse in post-war Britain than before, when off-the-peg styles dominated. Crucial to waste prevention, consumers were encouraged to make cloth-ing last. Circulated in 1943, and re-issued after the war, the Ministry of Information pamphlet, *Make Do and Mend*, informed British subjects that a pair of shoes lasts longer when alternated with another, because footwear 'benefits from a rest'. Clothes that are clean are clothes that endure. In these circumstances, it is unsurprising that second-hand fabrics commanded £10 per ton.[18] That is 10 times the value of salvaged glass, five times salvaged metal, and twice salvaged waste paper.[19]

---

[14] Zweiniger Bargielowska, n 10, 163. The author states that 80% of successful prosecu-tions resulted in fines of £5 or less, with 3–5% resulting in custodial sentences.

[15] P Hennessy, *Having it So Good: Britain in the Fifties* (Penguin 2007) 11, citing C Driver, *The British at Table* (Chatto and Windus 1983).

[16] *Public Cleansing* (November 1947) 120, cited in T Cooper, 'Challenging the "Refuse Revolution": War, Waste and the Rediscovery of Recycling 1900–1950' (2008) 81 *Historical Research* 710.

[17] M Wood, *We Wore What We'd Got: Women's Clothes in World War II* (Warwickshire Books 1989). Men seemed less bothered, except when it came to the rationing of trouser length, which precluded buying trousers with turn-ups (buying longer trousers and 'self-turning' being the preferred way around this rule) (Zweiniger Bargielowska, n 10, 92).

[18] See *Public Cleansing*, n 16.

[19] ibid.

Thus there does not seem to be any doubt that law and practice in the immediate post-war era was extremely waste preventative. Waste historian Timothy Cooper describes the contents of Britain's municipal refuse in the 1950s as follows:

> Even as late as the 1950s, domestic refuse still composed primarily of dust and cinders from household fires, both of which had their uses in either brick making or land reclamation. Refuse also contained rags, paper, and metals, which could be salvaged.[20]

This is not to say that waste disposal sites did not exist. However, they were not as much in demand after as before the war, because of rationing law and the culture of extreme thrift and resourcefulness supporting it.

B. Austerity and Affluence: A 'Waste Regime'?

What is less clear is the extent to which the law and practice that minimised waste in the 1940s and 1950s persisted. One school of thought is that it did not. Cooper is a proponent of that school, through his work charting the emergence of what he calls a 'waste regime'.[21] By this is meant a systematic policy-driven switch from emphasis on waste prevention and salvage to safe disposal, which entailed the acceptance of waste as necessary part of affluent society.

Cooper's appraisal suggests that Britain was following in the wake of the United States. A ubiquitous reference point in the historical literature is the trend-reflecting US magazine publication *Life*, which, in 1955, celebrated the benefits of 'throwaway living'.[22] The magazine *Time* returned to this theme recently:

> The idea, it seems, was that humans had entered a kind of wanton Golden Age, when cleaning up after ourselves was just one more quaint waste of time, and tossing more and more of our used-once items into the trash was another sign of modernity's relentless ascendancy over the drudgery of the past.[23]

---

[20] T Cooper, 'War on Waste: The Politics of Recycling in Post-War Britain 1950–1975' (2009) 20 *Capitalism, Nature, Socialism* 53, 55.

[21] ibid 59ff.

[22] 'Throwaway Living', *Life*, 1 August 1955.

[23] Ben Cosgrove, 'Throwaway Living: When Tossing Out Everything Was All the Rage' *Time*, 15 May 2014, available at http://time.com/3879873/throwaway-living-when-tossing-it-all-was-all-the-rage/.

The key here is the 'used-once' item, but did this trend catch on in Britain?[24]

Taking as a reference point a high-profile waste source in the US – discarded bottles – in 1971, Oregon became the first State to legislate for a deposit-and-refund container scheme to deal with the scourge of increasingly bottle-littered streets.[25] But legislation in Britain was not needed, owing to a voluntary deposit-and-refund scheme (established in 1913) overseen by the British Food and Drink Federation. With three-pence payable on the return of a standard beer or soft drink in the late 1960s and early 1970s, consumers had a reasonable incentive to keep containers in circulation. This was popular. Around it evolved an intriguing informal waste prevention network of children and voluntary sector workers, who scoured streets and car parks for beverage bottle discards that were in good enough shape to redeem.

Cooper sees evidence for the waste regime argument in the radical rhetoric of Friends of the Earth.[26] The Friends, he argues, were seeking a regime change, and from this is inferred a change to a *wasteful regime*.[27] Yet it is doubtful that opposition to waste at this time was counter-cultural, notwithstanding that this group considered itself 'radical'. For example, there is little leftist about Lady Emmet, who tabled a Parliamentary motion on salvage and reclamation in March 1970.[28] Emmet considered that resourcefulness with materials and associated prevention of waste was a 'virtue of our national character'.[29] She recalled with pride the war on waste on the 1940s:

> Those of us who went through that time will remember that we saved everything that was in any way usable. I looked up my war records and I found that in my county alone in one year we saved 15 tons of aluminium for Lord Beaverbrook's Spitfire appeal, mostly in bottle tops. Even now when I throw away an empty cotton reel I think of the noble Baroness, Lady Swanborough, and feel guilty, because under her impetus as head of

[24] For a critique of the US 'waste regime' in the five years after the *Time* article, see Vance Packard, *The Waste Makers* (David McKay 1960).

[25] Oregon Beverage Container Act 1971. This legislation was driven more by consideration of street aesthetics than resource conservation.

[26] Cooper, n 20, 60.

[27] ibid.

[28] 'Waste Material: Salvage and Reclamation', HL Deb, vol 308, 11 March 1970, cols 806–23. Lady Violet Emmet of Amberley Farm (and Castle) was a Tory peer who at the time was Deputy Speaker of the House of Lords.

[29] HL Deb, 11 March 1970, col 808.

the W.V.S. [Women's Volunteer Service] we collected thousands of cotton reels for the Air Force.[30]

This is not the language, nor is the House of Lords the place, of regime change. This is the British establishment speaking out against squandering resources.

Meredith Veldman depicts the Friends of the Earth campaign in a subtly different political light to Cooper, which comes closer to appreciating its 'establishment character'.[31] She situates the Cadbury Schweppes campaign within a romantic tradition railing against 'materialism'.[32] This is plausible, but it is inconsistent with Veldman's argument that the Friends of the Earth were dissenters.[33] The romantic tradition at this time was highly influential, and pervasive. It found expression not only in the major sources referred to by Veldman – such as CS Lewis or JRR Tolkien – but in mainstream secondary education, through the set texts of GM Trevelyan.[34] Beyond literature it took form in the popular high-street products of Laura Ashley and on television, the programmes broadcasting virtues of thrift, above all (with an early age audience in mind) *The Wombles*, first aired by the BBC a month into Britain's community membership.

The Friends of the Earth campaign thus tapped into what the Government described as the 'instinctive wrongness' of waste, in the Green Paper, *War on Waste*: 'We all instinctively feel that there is something wrong in a society which wastes and discards resources on the scale which we do today.'[35] The Government urged 'a new national effort to conserve and reclaim scarce resources – a war on waste that involves all sections of the community'.[36]

Cooper suggests that *War on Waste* took the side of Schweppes in the Friends of the Earth campaign.[37] Yet whilst it acknowledged a legitimate role for packaging to help conserve food (and resources), it agreed with

---

[30] ibid. The holes in cotton reels were used to hide messages to help prisoners of war escape.

[31] Veldman, n 1.

[32] See further M Weiner, *English Culture and the Decline of the Industrial Spirit, 1850–1980* (Cambridge University Press 1981).

[33] Veldman, n 1, 226 ('Friends of the Earth was an eco-activist, not a conservationist, organisation; it sought fundamental change').

[34] GM Trevelyan, *Illustrated English Social History*, vol 4 (Longman 1949). See too Weiner, n 32, 86–87, 132ff.

[35] Her Majesty's Government, *War on Waste: A Policy for Reclamation* Cm 5727 (HMSO 1974) [1.1] (hereinafter '*War on Waste*').

[36] ibid.

[37] Cooper, n 20, 70.

Friends of the Earth that it is absurdly costly in energy terms to recycle glass bottles (breaking them up and refabricating them) when the infrastructure is in place for re-use.[38] Thus, in its policy rhetoric, the British Government appears not to have abandoned the waste preventative ethos of the 1940s and 1950s. The language of 'War' suggests continuity. This is the social milieu in which Friends of the Earth impressed upon Lord Watkinson the need to be more British.

Finally, perhaps the best illustration of the establishment nature of the Friends of the Earth campaign is the Friends publication authored by Christine Thomas, called *Material Gains*:[39]

> 'Conservation' wrote John Kennedy, 'is the highest form of national thrift'. Thrift in Britain's use of materials – whether native or imported – is itself one commodity we can ill afford to discard.[40]

Leaving aside the interesting references to affluent society across the Atlantic, it is fascinating that it is not thrift but *national* thrift that is the concern.

Friends of the Earth, then, started out life performing the dual role of new pressure group and an old voluntary society, and the initial focus on waste can be understood as chosen because no aspect of environmental concerns at this time engaged as broad a consensus of resistance to modernisation as the growing amount of domestic waste, particularly paper. A year into Community membership, and before the Waste Framework Directive was proposed, the Friends teamed up with local church societies and the Boy Scouts to salvage 200,000 tonnes of scrap paper.[41] As Clapp points out, there was nothing new about scout groups and church societies being engaged with the war on waste.[42] What was new was that they were joined by a media-smart modern pressure group, which had faith in what Bugler described, scornfully, as the 'Whitehall Way or the Westminster Walk'.[43]

A year after *War on Waste*, the *Daily Mail* sponsored its annual 'Ideal Home Exhibition', with a variety of exhibits that reflected the thrifty

---

[38] *War on Waste*, n 35, 61.

[39] C Thomas, *Material Gains: Reclamation, Recycling and Re-Use* (Friends of the Earth 1974).

[40] ibid 2.

[41] Waste Management Advisory Council (WMAC), 1st Report (Department of Environment and Department of Industry 1976) 14.

[42] B Clapp, *An Environmental History of Britain* (Longman 1994) 190ff.

[43] J Bugler, 'Friends of the Earth is 10 Years Old', *New Scientist* (30 April 1981) 294, 296. Bugler is critical of this conservatism, describing it as 'glib, twee and … Fabian'.

national mood: 'wall lights made from empty tin cans, rugs from old cardigans, a lamp from cigarette packets, a chair from drainpipes, a table from corrugated iron sheeting'.[44]

C. Landfill

The emphasis placed on waste prevention meant that practice lower down the implicit waste hierarchy was neglected by regulatory law. This is particularly true of landfill, which the Department of Environment civil servant Martin Holdgate described as an ancient practice of particular interest to archaeologists, but not anything environmental activists need be concerned about:[45]

> Inevitably, the volume and complexity of ... wastes has increased in the modern industrial era, but most dumped materials are innocuous, and so long as they do not directly foul water supplies, they will have little effect on human health and well-being.[46]

The position of Friends of the Earth was that if waste could not be prevented and must be disposed of somehow, landfill was by far the most suitable mode for household waste: it was an effective means of facilitating the return of organic material (as most domestic waste was) to the soil, much preferable to incineration.[47] The Waste Management Advisory Committee added a further perspective when it sought to the define landfill as a form of reclamation – particularly of old mines, quarries and the foreshore.[48]

Landfill was barely addressed within regulatory law. Not until the Town and Country Planning Act 1947 was regulatory consent required to site and construct a landfill, and there was no regulation of the conduct of landfill until the Deposit of Poisonous Waste Act 1972 and

---

[44] Sandbrook, n 1, 212.

[45] M Holdgate, *A Perspective of Environmental Pollution* (Cambridge University Press 1979) 103.

[46] ibid.

[47] Thomas, n 39, 4. Department of Environment, *The Waste Landfill Research Technical Note 43* (HMO 1976) reported 'few cases' of contamination of public water supply and considered that leachate could be practicably controlled to avoid problems in future.

[48] WMAC, n 41, 16. 'This method of disposal [landfill] offers opportunities for reclaiming land. It is important that its value in this respect should not be overlooked and that over-cautious attitudes should not be allowed to force waste disposal authorities to more expensive methods of disposal when these offer neither economic nor environmental advantage.'

the Control of Pollution Act (COPA) 1974. Instead, waste disposal practice was regulated privately, such as through land law and tort.

According to the Dawes Report,[49] the emphasis on common law resulted in mixed standards. A notorious example of 'bad practice' was the tip at Hornchurch, London, which started out as a two-foot deep ditch that grew into a towering 90-foot high dump containing smouldering waste.[50] This can be juxtaposed to the landfill of the town of Bradford, established in 1923. It was an impressive feat of civil engineering, involving waste being disposed of in different cells, according to the combinations of waste that were most suitable for their position in the various strata. After the Second World War, the 'Bradford system' became the orthodoxy. By the time Britain joined the Community, 85 per cent of waste was disposed of by means of controlled landfill.[51]

There are a number of explanations for the dominance of landfill. Whilst landfills have always been, to borrow from the environmental justice literature, 'locally unwanted land-uses' in Britain, as elsewhere, they have tended to be viewed by local populations as the lesser of two evils compared to incineration. Britain had a lot of experience of incineration in the early days of public cleansing.[52] The ominously named destructors (incinerators), which were the mode of disposal of choice in late Victorian and Edwardian Britain, and even as late as the 1930s, were attractive to local authorities because they afforded recovery of energy from the waste. But clean air campaigners objected to them,[53] and local authorities ran the gauntlet of the threat of nuisance litigation. There does not seem to have been an organised campaign against landfill. Good practice evolved through the industry body the Institute of Public Cleansing. The Government's technical advisers endorsed the Bradford system: performed professionally, landfill was usually the best practicable environmental option.[54]

With landfill now the orthodoxy, central government turned attention to its regulation. In one of his final acts as Environment Minister,

[49] A Report of an Investigation of Public Cleansing Services in the Administrative County of London (HMSO 1929) (Dawes Report).
[50] ibid 30. The Hornchurch tip had been receiving up to 350,000 tonnes per annum of London waste since the turn of the century.
[51] WMAC, n 41, 16.
[52] By 1912, 300 destructors were in operation, 76 of which were used to generate power. P Williams, *Waste Treatment and Disposal* (Wiley 1998) 2.
[53] E Ashby and M Anderson, *Politics of Clean Air* (Cambridge University Press 1981). See further ch 5 of this book.
[54] Department of Environment, *Cooperative Programme of Research on the Behaviour of Hazardous Wastes in Landfill: Policy Review Committee Final Report* (HMSO 1978).

Tony Crosland appointed two working parties to report on the scope for the introduction of regulatory laws: one focused on disposal of hazardous (toxic) waste, the other on household waste.[55] These recommended the introduction of a 'cradle to grave' system of criminal administrative controls over waste management practices, including a duty on local authorities to survey their areas and record waste arisings (quantity and quality), and a system of prior approval of landfill operations accompanied by conditions aimed at protecting drinking water, public health and amenity. The Deposit of Poisonous Waste Act 1972 was rushed through Parliament to implement the first of these reports, after sodium cyanide was found dumped in a disused brickworks in Warwickshire.[56] Part I of the COPA 1974 followed once the Local Government Act 1972 had started to bed in. A key part of this was the introduction, within the new local government structures, of formal waste disposal authority surveys of waste and opportunities for re-use and recycling, looking forward 10 years.[57]

Hence, Britain entered the Community with a body of regulatory law addressed to 'special waste' (hazardous waste) and 'controlled waste' more generally, which it intended to bring into force in stages. These public law controls were superimposed on a private law framework, and a wider sense of civic duty and goodwill (reflected in national pressure groups working alongside older local organisations). The immediate priority of the Government was to gather, for the first time, information about national waste arisings, so that it would no longer have to fall back on vague statements such as these, taken from the First Report of the Waste Management Advisory Committee:

> Households, shops and offices produce about 18 million tonnes of waste a year.
>
> Industry produces much greater quantities of waste but a lot of this is reused in either the parent or some other manufacturing process; about 23 million tonnes a year remain for disposal.
>
> Large quantities of waste arise from agriculture and forestry but much of this is immediately used on the land and no reliable figures are available.[58]

---

[55] Department of Environment, *Report of the Technical Committee on the Disposal of Solid Toxic Waste Disposal* (HMSO 1970); Department of Environment, *Report of the Working Party on Refuse Disposal* (HMSO 1971).

[56] The 1972 Act was replaced in 1980 by the Control of Pollution (Special Waste) Regulations 1980 (SI 1980/1709), made under s 17 of COPA1974.

[57] COPA 1974, Pt I, esp ss 1–2. Department of the Environment, *Waste Management Paper No 3, Guidelines for the Preparation of Waste Disposal Plans* (HMSO 1976).

[58] WMAC, n 41, 7.

Per capita household waste by weight does not appear to have grown between 1945 and 1973.[59] In other words, Britain was operating at or near the top of the implicit waste hierarchy when its EU journey began.

II. THE BRITISH WAY OF WASTE DURING EU MEMBERSHIP

Britain, alongside Germany and France, provided the model for the Waste Framework Directive 1975.[60] These three countries were enacting, or in Britain's case had recently enacted, regulatory laws tackling various aspects of the subject. The phrase 'waste hierarchy', though not explicit in the Directive, is implicit in the requirement that Member States shall take appropriate steps to *encourage* the prevention and recycling of waste,[61] whilst *ensuring* that waste is safely disposed of by appointing competent authorities with duties to plan, organise, authorise and supervise waste disposal operations.[62] This concern with the whole cycle of waste, from generation through to disposal, is reflected in the change in the initial title of the Directive (which focused on 'Waste Disposal') to one concerning 'Waste' more broadly, as agreed.[63] A notable aspect of the Directive is its ease of passage through the legislative process. Within 10 months of the initial proposal the Directive was agreed. The British Environment Minister (Denis Howell) accounted for this in terms of the persuasiveness of the case for modelling it on COPA 1974.[64] Nigel Haigh wrote that COPA 1974 was an attractive template for harmonisation from a Community perspective because it was both new and comprehensive.[65]

---

[59] If the figure of 18m tonnes is divided equally into household waste, on the one hand, and shop and office waste, on the other, that gives a per capita household waste arising of 170kg. The growth was in volume, not weight, with lesser amounts of heavy fire waste (ash, cinders) and more amounts of light, bulky waste (cardboard and plastic packaging). Recycling seems high. The biggest stream was paper (33%), followed by 'fine material' of under 20mm (19%), vegetable and putrescible material (18%), metal (10%), glass (10%), rag (3.5%), plastics (1.5%). The remaining 5% was miscellaneous materials (ibid).

[60] EEC Directive 75/442 on Waste [1975] OJ L194/39.

[61] ibid, Art 3.

[62] This is the combined effect of Arts 4 and 5.

[63] N Haigh, *EEC Environmental Policy: An Essay and Handbook* (ENDS Data Services 1984) 131.

[64] 'I think we can claim that here the EEC was following our Control of Pollution Act … [the Directive] is a very enlightened and acceptable document' (cited ibid).

[65] ibid 303, contrasting waste with other sectors: 'The incremental character of British policy on water and air makes it look unsystematic when viewed from outside and unattractive to the Commission draftsman. In contrast, the waste part of the Control of Pollution

This consensus, which is in marked contrast to the contested character of Community regulation in the field of water considered in chapter 4, held firm until two controversies surrounding a shift in Community waste policy and law in the late 1980s. One controversy centred on the Commission's proposal for a Directive on Civil Liability for Damage Caused by Waste, to which most countries had objections of principle because it concerned harmonisation of private law.[66] Each Member State had either subtle and/or not so subtle doctrinal and procedural differences in this field, with differences both within the civilian law paradigm, and between that and the common law paradigm of Britain and the Irish Republic. Britain's negotiators saw the proposed Directive as a threat to the common law of nuisance (delict in Scotland), as grounded in a wider common law constitution protecting rights (and responsibilities) in respect of property in land.[67] There is a suggestion in the literature that the proposal could have garnered the support of a majority, and have been passed under the qualified majority voting procedure without Britain's support, but that the Council 'fought shy'.[68] The proposal was dropped.

A second, deeper controversy centred on the Commission's proposal for a Landfill Directive, which was eventually agreed at Community level without Britain's approval).[69] This is the focus of much of the remainder of the chapter. As Nigel Haigh explains,[70] the principal background

Act, for the very reason that it was so original, is much more coherent and lent itself being turned into Community legislation'. See further chs 4–6 of this book.

[66] M Wilde, *Civil Liability for Environmental Damage: Comparative Analysis of Law and Policy in Europe and the US* (Kluwer 2013) 192–95. The author comments that 'states are typically reluctant to alter domestic liability rules in a manner which may undermine sovereignty' (ibid 195). On the strong policy wish to preserve common law rules, see House of Lords Select Committee on the European Communities, *Paying for Pollution – Civil Liability for Damage Caused by Waste*, 25th Report Session 1989–1990 (HLP 1990); House of Lords Select Community, *Remedying Environmental Damage*, Third Report Session 1993–1994 (HLP 1993).

[67] House of Lords Select Committee on the European Communities, *Paying for Pollution – Civil Liability for Damage Caused by Waste* (above n 67). On the centrality of common law property (rights) to the British constitution, see *Entick v Carrington* (1765) 95 ER 807, and the discussion of its legacy in A Tomkins and P Scott (eds), *Entick v Carrington: 250 Years of the Rule of Law* (Hart Publishing 2015).

[68] M Hedemann-Robinson and M Wilde, 'Towards a European Tort Law on the Environment? European Union Initiatives and Developments on Civil Liability in Respect of Environmental Harm' in J Lowry and R Edmunds (eds), *Environmental Protection and the Common Law* (Hart Publishing 2000) 201, 235.

[69] Directive 1999/31/EC on the Landfill of Waste [1999] OJ L182/1.

[70] N Haigh, *EU Environmental Policy: Its Journey to the Centre Stage* (Routledge 2016) 69ff.

to the Landfill Directive lies in German reunification, which brings the histories of British and EU law back to the immediate post-war period. In the 1960s and 1970s, Germany's waste policy switched from emphasis on incineration to landfill (landfilling in practice 70 per cent of waste).[71] With landfill costs rising as space for sites became increasingly limited, the country looked across the Berlin Wall for additional disposal capacity. This led to what soon became Europe's largest landfill, at Schönberg/ Ihlenberg, where a large quantity of German waste was disposed of cheaply and without the regulatory constraints of the Waste Framework Directive. A unified Germany had no hope of complying with the Directive in these circumstances. Thus German politicians started to pursue what Stephen Tromans calls 'aggressive policies on recycling'.[72] This was reflected in legislation radically changing the domestic waste regulatory regime drafted in 1989 (and enacted in 1994).[73]

Under the revised German waste law, practice reverted to incineration as the dominant mode of disposal, with an emphasis on recycling as a means of keeping within the country's own disposal capacity.[74] The emergence of recycling in Germany (and other countries) presented the Commission with a dilemma concerning the relationship between environmental protection and freedom of movement of goods and services. It blurred the boundary between 'waste' (as something of no economic value to dispose of) and 'resource' (as a commodity which engaged the Community's economic freedoms. The Commission had recently taken proceedings against Denmark in respect of its 'highly effective' deposit-and-return scheme for bottles and cans – effective in that it enabled containers which would otherwise be single use to be used up to 30 times.[75] The scheme resembled that operating in Britain with which the chapter began, insofar as it originated in an informal initiative between consumers and businesses. The differences is that it was put on a statutory footing by the Danish legislature in 1978, and made tougher (or more restrictive in terms of freedom of movement) in 1981 and 1984.

---

[71] R Stokes, R Koster and C Sambrook, *Business of Waste: Great Britain and Germany, 1945–Present* (Cambridge University Press 2013) 280.

[72] S Tromans, 'EC Waste Law – A Complete Mess?' (2001) 13 *Journal of Environmental Law* 133, 135.

[73] Closed Substance Cycle and Waste Management Act 1994. S Hempen and F Jager, 'Germany's New Waste Management Act – Towards the Management of Material Flows and Closed Substance Cycles' (1995) 4 *European Environmental Law Review* 138.

[74] ibid; and Stokes et al, above n 71.

[75] *Commission v Denmark*, Case No 302/86, 20 September 1988 (1990) 2 *Journal of Environmental Law* 89, Opinion of the Advocate General, Sir Gordon Slynn, ibid 94.

Whilst the European Court of Justice (ECJ) upheld the legality of the 1978 and 1981 schemes, it impugned the 1984 version. Denmark, it was reasoned, had not established the proportionality of the scheme's inter-ference with freedom of movement of goods.[76]

The Commission's decision to take proceedings against Denmark understandably generated heavy criticism within the national (Danish) and wider European green movement. Environmental activists in Denmark called for a repatriation of exclusive environmental compe-tence in the waste field. Re-nationalisation was further mooted as a solution to the problems arising from German reunification. The case grew stronger with the agreement of new international waste law,[77] which enabled an inter-governmental approach to waste that was attractive to Member States including Britain. In these circumstances the Commission confronted, as Ludwig Kramer notes, a stark choice between 'renational-ising' of waste provision,[78] and embracing EU competence and pushing forward with a new waste policy and law, to address the changing politi-cal and legal framework in Europe and internationally. It chose the latter option.[79]

In the event, most of the Commission's new initiatives sat well with British way thinking. In particular, the amendment of the Waste Framework Directive in 1991 to make the waste hierarchy explicit[80] had, the British Government considered, been foreshadowed by domes-tic regulatory reforms under the Environmental Protection Act 1990. Likewise, Community intervention in the field of packaging seemed to be an opportunity for Britain to pass on the benefit of its experi-ence in this field.[81] More recently, the EU's circular economy package of measures has been well received in Britain, particularly the waste prevention programmes provided for under the latest Waste Framework

[76] P Kromarek, 'Analysis' (1990) 2 *Journal of Environmental Law* 96, 105, commented that the ECJ decision rendered the 1984 law 'almost otiose'.

[77] The Basel Convention on the Control of Transboundary Movements of Hazardous Waste and their Disposal 1989 (1989) 28 *ILM* 657.

[78] L Kramer, *Focus on European Environmental Law*, 2nd edn (Sweet & Maxwell 1997) 333. Officials of France and, tellingly, Britan advocated this position.

[79] Albeit that the Commission was, Kramer acknowledges, 'relatively open' to renation-alisation; it was a close call: see L Kramer, 'EU Environmental Law and Policy Over the Last 25 Years – Good or Bad for the UK?' (2013) 25 *Environmental Law and Management* 48, 54.

[80] EC Directive 1991/156/EC amending Directive 1975/442 [1991] OJ L78/32.

[81] 'Ministers Accept Industry Demands for Packaging Waste Legislation' (1994) 236 ENDS 12.

Directive 2008.[82] Britain's enthusiastic compliance with this tool of prevention has been acknowledged in the literature.[83]

However, legislative proposals for regulating landfill met with trenchant opposition by a small minority of Member States which included Britain.[84] The idea behind the proposed Landfill Directive was to divert biodegradable waste away from landfill, in order to encourage recycling of it,[85] as well as to require the pre-treatment of certain waste prior to landfilling, so as to further encourage the identification and separation of recyclable material and to limit 'risky' co-disposal.[86] Britain saw this as an attack on its national way, which revolved around co-disposal, and therefore its sovereignty in environmental matters. Moreover, it saw the proposal as prejudicing Britain economically, by preventing the country from taking full advantage of its relatively landfill-favourable hydrogeological conditions.

The British Government's position was underpinned by thorough consideration through various technical departmental reports,[87] which found co-disposal to be a 'valuable and environmentally sound method of disposal'.[88] Most influential was the inquiry of the Royal Commission on Environmental Pollution (RCEP), which reported that landfill was the prima facie Best Practicable Environmental Option for all materials other than those that are volatile or flammable (which should generally be incinerated).[89]

---

[82] Art 29 and Annex IV, Directive 2008/98/EC on Waste [2008] OJ L312/3.

[83] J Malinauskaite, H Jouhara and N Spencer, 'Waste Prevention and Technologies in the Context of the EU Waste Framework Directive: Lost in Translation?' (2017) 26 *European Energy and Environmental Law Review* 66, 76.

[84] EC Directive 99/31 on the Landfill of Waste [1999] OJ L182/1. For a history of the drafting of the Directive, see M Forster, 'The Landfill Directive: How Will the UK Meet the Challenge?' (2000) 9 *European Environmental Law Review* 16. For the Commission's intended encouragement of a switch from landfill to incineration as the normal mode of disposal, see C Glinski and P Rott, 'Waste Incineration – Legal Protection in European Environmental Law' (2000) 12 *Journal of Environmental Law* 129, 130.

[85] Art 5 requires Member States to devise national strategies for the reduction of biodegradable municipal waste going to landfill to 75% of the 1995 total by 2006; 50% by 2009; and 35% by 2016. Britain negotiated an option of postponing the 2016 deadline by four years (Forster, n 84, 17).

[86] Art 6.

[87] See eg Department of Environment Waste Technical Division, *A Review of Technical Aspects of Co-Disposal*, WM/007/89 (DOE 1989). See Williams, n 52, 223–29.

[88] E Bramwell, 'UK Government Policy' (1994) 3 *European Environmental Law Review* 44, 45.

[89] Royal Commission on Environmental Pollution, *Managing Waste: The Duty of Care*, 11th Report, Cm 9675 (HMSO 1985) 42. See also *A Review of Technical Aspects of Co-Disposal*, n 87.

Whilst the Commission persisted with its policy of harmonisation away from co-disposal in the face of this opposition, its ambition was frustrated by a difference of opinion between the European Parliament and the Council about how 'strict' the Directive should be. Members of the European Parliament (MEPs) generally favoured a speedy end to landfill throughout the Community, and pushed for a radical reform to Community waste law. The Council advocated a more flexible approach, cognisant of the British position, and a handful of Member States who also favoured landfill for reasons ground in established national practice. However, the Commission continued to push it policy of harmonisation, indicating that it would seek to secure to agreement on the basis of a qualified majority if necessary.

Unable to rely on a veto, Britain set about the task of garnering support from other Member States. The Government had the support of Ireland and Portugal, for whom landfill was the strongly preferred option. But that was not enough. It needed support of at least one more Member State. The machinations are captured in the following coverage by the ENDS Report:

> The main waverers are Finland, which can ultimately be expected to side with its two Nordic partners [Denmark and Sweden, both supporters of the Directive], and Spain, which has no strong commitment and can possibly be persuaded to vote for [the Directive] by the promise of a sufficient lead in period and structural fund cash.[90]

And so it transpired. The proposal was passed without the votes of Britain, Ireland and Portugal.

The analysis immediately above concerns *Community* environmental governance. However, the negotiations around the proposed Directive also highlight an important aspect of environmental governance the Westminster way. When occupying the constitutional role of Her Majesty's loyal opposition, under the leadership of Tony Blair, the Labour Party impressed upon the British Government the merits of a hard line on landfill. That was also the view of Friends of the Earth, with whom Shadow Environment Secretary Michael Meacher worked closely. The Friends considered that the requirement to treat waste prior to disposal would, as intended, stimulate recycling (by making disposal more expensive). They thus welcomed the Commission's attempt to move EU law up the waste hierarchy, subject to the reservation that the Directive might encourage many countries to burn rather than dump

---

[90] 'UK to be Put on the Spot by New Landfill Proposal' [1996] 261 ENDS Report 36, 37.

waste, and that could be disastrous.[91] In a classic exercise of institution-
alised Parliamentary opposition, the Shadow Environment Secretary
urged the Government to embrace the Landfill Directive.[92]

What makes this opposition illuminating from a domestic governance perspective is what happened when the Labour Party formed the
new government in 1997, and the Directive still had not been agreed.
Now Secretary of State for the Environment, Meacher changed tack and
adopted the policy of the previous Conservative administration. This
policy was formulated in cooperation with the Environmental Services
Association (ESA) (as the Edwardian 'Public Cleansing Institute' was by
then known), representing the domestic waste management industry.[93]
ESA described the proposed Directive as 'totally inappropriate'.[94]
Britain's waste managers, it reasoned, deserved respect for the
professionalism with which they conducted landfill operations. Thus
Meacher complained that the Commission's proposals 'do not show
sufficient regard for subsidiarity, or for Member States to adopt their
own, environmentally sustainable, waste management systems, in light
of their own national circumstances'.[95]

This, then, is a story of fine political margins. As Community law
evolved from the broad framework type legislation of the early days
underpinned by consensus decision making, to more prescriptive regulation underpinned by qualified majority voting, there was always a
prospect that a British way argument might be lost, as feared by early
critics of Community competence in the environmental sphere. In the
event, the 'loss of control' did not have the regressive practical impact
that some predicted. The Directive did not encourage a switch in Britain
away from landfill to incineration. That was not considered responsible,
or politically attractive. But it did result in the Government's change of
plans for the disposal of 2.2 million tonnes of waste that it could no
longer landfill the British way. The cost of disposing of this waste under
the Directive was estimated by the Government at £100 per tonne, or
double that of its nationally preferred policy.[96]

---

[91] Ibid. See too Forster, n 84, 20.

[92] T Heppel (ed), *Leaders of the Opposition from Churchill to Cameron* (Palgrave
Macmillan 2012) 2.

[93] It called the proposed Directive 'totally unacceptable': 'EC Waste Strategy Jars with
UK on Landfills, Waste Hierarchy' [1996] 255 ENDS Report 43, 44.

[94] Ibid 44.

[95] 'Business Much as Usual as UK Objects to Landfill Directive' [1997] 271 ENDS
Report 30.

[96] Ibid, n 95, 31.

The episode placed strain on British and EU relations, and on relations between Britain and the Member State seen as driving the law for self-serving ends (Germany). Consider, for example, the disparaging remarks directed at German waste policy by the British Parliament.[97] Furthermore, more subtly, it added to the distance between the Friends of the Earth and the domestic establishment. The early consensus that landfill was the most suitable mode of disposal as a general rule in Britain included the Friends, whose campaign strategy was to move comfortably in Westminster and Whitehall circles. Following the Single European Act 1986, that strategy altered, as some emphasis shifted onto pressure being put on Community institutions. That is important context to the appraisal of Brexit in this field as 'very high risk', which refers to the risk of the Landfill Directive being diluted when its legal status moves from being binding EU law to nationally amendable 'retained law'.

In defence of the argument that leaving the EU acquis in this area is dangerous, there is no doubt that the British way relies upon political will both at a governmental level, and at a grassroots one, and that it is vulnerable to fluctuation. The period between the enactment of COPA 1974 and Part II of the Environmental Protection Act 1990 was one of undeniable decline in political momentum behind the war on waste. Key provisions of COPA concerning recycling were never brought into force, and those that were were poorly administered.[98] The regime, it was found (in a series of Westminster Parliamentary inquiries), was nowhere near to delivering the cradle-to-grave regime revolving around waste surveys, waste plans and licensing decisions, which would keep 'waste' as a resource and, as a last resort, ensure its safe disposal. In statistical terms, household recycling under COPA was never more than 5 per cent per annum nationally, and some local authorities made absolutely no provision for recycling.[99] The quantity of household waste collected by local authorities had grown from about 10 to 20 million tonnes. Britain

[97] See the House of Lords Select Committee on Sustainable Development, commenting on Germans 'falling flat on their faces on recycling', which is a reference to the decision in the early 1990s to build 15 new incinerators to dispose of plastic that had been collected for recycling but for which there was no market (House of Lords Select Committee on Sustainable Development, Evidence, Q1716, Waste Watch).

[98] S Bell, D McGillivray, O Pedersen, E Lees and E Stokes, *Environmental Law*, 9th edn (Oxford University Press 2017) 660–62. The industry as a whole had the feel of a 'Cinderella service': House of Commons Environment Committee, *Toxic Waste*, Second Report 1988–1989 (HC 22).

[99] Her Majesty's Government, *This Common Inheritance: Britain's Environmental Strategy*, Cm 1200 (HMSO 1990).

entered the Community at war on waste, but soon became among the more wasteful Member States.[100]

Against this backdrop it is understandable that Friends of the Earth moved away from a waste campaign that revolved around the branding of waste as 'unBritish' to one focusing on shaming the country for being the dirty man of Europe. And it is unsurprising that Community institutions were now an attractive forum for the group's campaigning. Key to the environmental case in favour of as soft a Brexit as possible is the performance of Britain under the reformed Community waste regime. Britain since the early 1990s has embraced recycling and waste prevention, with the practical upshot that, in 2015, 43 per cent of all municipal waste was recycled.[101] This is the ninth highest rate within the EU (Germany being highest on 66 per cent).[102] Furthermore, per capita waste declined from over 500kg per annum in the early 2000s to 483kg per annum in 2016.[103] Of the EU-9, only Belgium now produces less waste per capita than Britain. Germany, in contrast, produces 627kg, which is the third highest (behind Denmark and Cyprus).

But is this a consequence of Community intervention? My argument is that it is a consequence of the persistence of the British way. Britain is leaving the EU with an increasingly positive environmental profile in this field because of pressure from *domestic* institutions. Dependence on domestic political will is the key strength of the British way, because it revolves around domestic institutions which have the capability of pointing out troubles, identifying solutions and ensuring the solutions are implemented. In the case of waste, weaknesses in the implementation of COPA 1974 were an affront to the Crown in Parliament which had enacted it. The job of exposing that lay with committees of MPs and peers, whose reports set in train reforms under Part II of the Environmental Protection Act 1990, with a fresh emphasis on recycling,

---

[100] Comparative data for 1995, 2000 and 2005 reveal Britain to be above average in the among of domestic waste its households produce: Eurostat, 'Municipal Waste Generated by Countries in Selected Years' (European Commission 2018), available at http://ec.europa.eu/eurostat/statistics-explained/index.php?title=File:Municipal_waste_generated_by_country_in_selected_years_(kg_per_capita)_.png.

[101] European Environment Agency, *Recycling of Municipal Waste* (EEA 2017).

[102] Within Britain and Northern Ireland, Wales stands out at rate of 64%, making it comparable to Germany. See eg Sandra Laville, 'Wales is Second Best Household Recycler in the World', *The Guardian* (11 December 2017).

[103] Eurostat, 'Municipal Waste Generated by Countries in Selected Years', n 100. See further the suggestion that the landfill tax has played an important part in reducing waste, in Her Majesty's Government, *A Green Future: Our 25 Year Plan to Improve the Environment* (Crown Copyright 2018) 83.

and underpinned by a renewed emphasis on prevention. Crucially, this Parliamentary effort created a climate in which the first national environment strategy for two decades – *This Common Inheritance* – stated that 'the first priority is to reduce waste at source to a minimum'.[104] Included within this was the policy target of recycling half all 'recyclable waste' by 2000.[105] This was achieved (albeit in 2005).[106] *This Common Inheritance* also contained a policy of stabilising household waste arising, which was the cornerstone of the national Waste Strategy of 2005.[107] This too has been achieved.

III. CONCLUSION

In a speech entitled 'The Unfrozen Moment – Delivering a Green Brexit',[108] Environment Secretary Michael Gove catalogued threats to the environment which have become more acute since the enactment of the European Communities Act 1972, with waste to the fore: '[W]e've allowed extractive and exploitative political systems to lay waste to natural resources'. Whilst Gove acknowledges that Community membership has been beneficial in some respects, the 'unfrozen moment' motif suggests that Britain's environment today, for good or ill, owes itself to EU membership. On that reasoning, Brexit is a new opportunity, which has not existed for decades, to take control of environmental policy and law. On that basis, Gove has announced eye catching new policy initiatives such as the objective of 'zero avoidable waste' by 2050, with a similar but earlier target for plastics (2042).[109] Also in this rubric of an unleashed domestic independence is the deposit and refund scheme the Government is now thinking of legislating for.[110]

---

[104] *This Common Inheritance*, above n 99, [14.3].

[105] ibid [14.23]. This equated to a target of 25%.

[106] Local Authority Collected Waste Management Statistics: Overall Recycling Rates 2000–2015 (Crown Copyright 2016).

[107] Department of Environment, *Making Waste Work: A Strategy for Sustainable Waste Management in England and Wales*, Cm 3040 (HMSO 1995).

[108] M Gove, 'The Unfrozen Moment – Delivering a Green Brexit', 21 July 2017 https://www.gov.uk/government/speeches/the-unfrozen-moment-delivering-a-green-brexit.

[109] Her Majesty's Government, *Clean Growth Strategy: Leading the Way to a Low Carbon Future* (Crown Copyright 2017) 108. This is about *practicable* waste prevention: 'Zero avoidable waste equates to eliminating all waste where it is technically, environmentally and economically practicable to do so.'

[110] D Carrington, 'Bottle and Can Deposit Refund Scheme get the Green Light in England', *The Guardian* (27 March 2018). Similar legislation at the time of writing is planned by Scotland's Government.

Westminster MP Caroline Lucas' response to this scheme further echoes to theme of policy released from being 'on hold': 'After a long delay it is good to see the government moving forward on this issue. This scheme should have been introduced long ago'.[111]

The argument in this chapter, however, is that the European Communities Act 1972 did not place the British way into abeyance. The British way has continued to protect the environment in the field of waste throughout EU membership. Waste illustrates the persistence of the British way as a sword, in so far as EU framework waste legislation of the present day is modelled on COPA 1974. The 1975 Waste Framework Directive occupies a unique place in this history of the EU environmental acquis: it was the first Community measure to be explicitly grounded in a combination of pollution prevention and resource conservation objectives – the first, as it were, *environmental* Directive. As a 'shield', the British way is evident in resistance to the draft Civil Liability for Waste Directive and (unsuccessfully) the Landfill Directive. The Landfill Directive can be viewed as a costly mistake not only for Britain, but the EU. This is because it encapsulates the idea of rigid harmonisation and insensitivity to national sentiments that has contributed to the outcome of the 2016 Referendum.

[111] ibid.

4

Rivers

W HEN BRITAIN ENTERED the European Community, the rivers of England and Wales had been subject to comprehensive surveys, measuring their quality and classifying that quality into four classes.[1] The survey of 1958 recorded 87.2 per cent of rivers as either 'unpolluted' (class 1) or 'mildly polluted' (class 2); in 1970, that had improved to 90.9 per cent, and in 1972, 92 per cent. This improving performance was understood as a reflection of investment in cleaner riparian technology on the part of sewage undertakings and trades discharging to watercourses, within the framework of a subtle mix of regulatory law and common law which the Ashby Report considered to exemplify the British way.[2] Commenting on the challenges ahead in the aftermath of the Stockholm Conference, Secretary of State Peter Walker emphasised the need to tackle the rump: the 1,000 miles of river (4.3 per cent) that were 'grossly polluted' (class 4), signifying that they were incapable of sustaining fish. To that end – and to maintain the wholesomeness of most watercourses – the Government was sponsoring the Water Bill 1972, which would create 10 regional water authorities with a mandate to pursue integrated river basin management, covering abstraction, navigation, drinking water supply, sewage (and its treatment) and regulation of discharges from riparian industry.

The subject matter of this chapter is widely considered among the most 'established' areas of EU environmental policy and law. Writing in the late 1980s, Johnson and Corcelle called it 'the oldest and most

---

[1] Ministry of Housing and Local Government, *River Pollution Survey*, National Archives, HLG 133/45 (1958); Department of Environment, *River Pollution Survey 1970*, vol 1 (HMSO 1971); Department of Environment, *River Pollution Survey Update* (HMSO 1972). The classes ranged from unpolluted (class 1) through to grossly polluted (class 4), with mildly polluted and more polluted in between (classes 2 and 3 respectively).

[2] E Ashby et al, *Pollution: Nuisance or Nemesis* (HMSO 1972) ('Ashby Report') 58–61. As noted in ch 2, rivers pollution regulation was singled out in the Report as the exemplum of 'the British way of environmental protection: each case on its merits').

complete sector of Community Environmental Policy'.[3] However, these early interventions were contentious from a British perspective. The country's negotiators were not persuaded that Community legislation was necessary, and disagreed with the inflexible (it was thought) regulatory style emerging from the European Commission. This had a 'downstream' effect in diminishing wider Member State appetite for implementing the law, which led to the European Commission's taking proceedings in the late 1980s against all 12 Member States, for systematic failure to implement the Dangerous Substances in Water Directive 1976 – the measure around which Britain's objections crystallised

The early controversy prompted an overhaul of Community policy and law, which culminated in the Water Framework Directive 2000 (WFD).[4] The WFD requires Member States to pursue integrated water environment management within river basin administrative structures, with the objective of all 'water bodies' in river basins being of 'good status'.[5] The WFD has been described as 'somewhere near the "high watermark" of Community environmental legislation both in terms of its general ambitiousness and in respect of its innovative qualities'.[6] According to Friends of the Earth, leaving the WFD and its supporting governance structures is, in the field of water quality, 'the principal area of concern'.[7] It is an area of 'high risk'.[8]

---

[3] S Johnson and G Corcelle, *The Environmental Policy of the European Communities* (Graham and Trotman 1989) 25. Ludwig Kramer began his exposition of substantive environmental law with what he called 'the wide range of provisions for the protection and improvement of the aquatic environment' (L Kramer, *EEC Treaty and Environmental Protection* (Sweet & Maxwell 1990) 3–8. Nigel Haigh started 'Handbook' section with the aquatic environment: N Haigh, *European Community Environmental Policy and Britain: An Essay and a Handbook* (ENDS Data Services 1984) (hereinafter '*Essay and Handbook*') 58–122.

[4] European Parliament and Council Directive 2000/60/EC Establishing a Framework for Community Action in the field of Water Policy [2000] OJ L327/1.

[5] See, eg, the definition of 'good ecological status' in Art 2(22) and Annex V. For a critique that is returned to below (n 90 and associated text) see H Josefsson and L Baaner, 'Water Framework Directive – A Directive for the Twenty-First Century?' (2011) 26 *Journal of Environmental Law* 463.

[6] W Howarth, 'Aspirations and Realities under the Water Framework Directive: Proceduralisation, Participation and Practicalities' (2009) 21 *Journal of Environmental Law* 391. For Elli Louka it is 'revolutionary' (E Louka, *Waste Law and Policy: Governance Without Frontier* (Oxford University Press 2008). A report for the World Wide Fund for Nature describes it 'as the most significant piece of EU environmental legislation ever introduced': T Le Quesne and C Green, *Can We Afford Not To? The Costs and Benefits of a Partnership Approach to the Water Framework Directive* (WWF 2005) 4.

[7] C Burns, V Gravey and A Jordan, *UK Environmental Policy Post-Brexit: A Risk Assessment* (Friends of the Earth 2017) 25.

[8] ibid.

The analysis in this chapter takes a different view of the prospects. The WFD is certainly a substantial advance on the initial Community interventions. Integrated river basin management and the emphasis on an overarching qualitative standard ('good') offer a British way-shaped legal framework worth retaining once Britain leaves the EU. In one important respect, however, the EU law is profoundly inconsistent with the British way. This is a reference to 'good status' being defined inflexibly and unrealistically, as a decline in performance against one parameter entails a negative assessment of the water body as a whole. Leaving the EU is an opportunity to work with a more holistic domestic measure of the quality of watercourses, which recognises that most rivers are 'up to standard' in their sustenance of aquatic flora and fauna and 'wholesomeness'.

I. THE BRITISH WAY OF RIVER QUALITY PROTECTION 1945–73

The British way of protecting river quality, as the country entered the European Community, is something that evolved throughout the posr-war period, based on lessons learned from the experience of weaknesses in earlier policy and law 'foundations'. It is characterised by a subtle and at times highly contentious mix of common law property provision and overlying regulatory law. Section I.A addresses regulatory law, highlighting a shift from a domestic regime geared around a paradigm of outright prohibition of river pollution to a more pragmatic one of control, geared around river basins and the reconciliation of their competing anthropogenic uses. Section I.B address the common law of riparian rights, and its relationship with regulatory law. Section I.C and I.D elaborate on the improvements in river quality in the post-war decades before Britain joined the EU, which I argue are attributable to the British way.

A. Regulatory Law – From Prevention to Control

The rivers (and broader watercourses) of immediate post-war Britain were regulated in criminal-administrative terms through the Rivers Pollution Prevention Act 1876. On paper it provided a public interest system of regulation, protecting the quality of the nation's watercourses for the benefit if all. The common law of riparian rights proved useful in protecting the quality of rivers of the *countryside*, where most people lived and worked, and where the British landed establishment showed a willingness to use nuisance law injunct 'industrial' polluters who interfered with the quality of rivers running through estates. But the common law was impotent in the face of pollution, in urban areas, where riparian ownership was dominated by polluting factories.[9]

Yet in practice the Act was rarely enforced in urban areas, because pollution was difficult to attribute to an individual wrongdoer (factories lined town and city river banks, their discharges mingling). Rather, enforcement was mainly in rural areas, where it was least needed, but where successful prosecutions were easiest to secure. There is a real possibility that the Act's enforcement practices unwittingly zoned pollution into urban areas, facilitating ghettos of pollution which the urban poor were expected to tolerate for the job opportunities which they reflected.[10] The Act became an icon of regulatory failure or, rather, of the futility of legislating out of existence systemic industrial pollution.[11]

The 1876 Act was repealed and replaced by the the Rivers (Prevention of Pollution) Act 1951.[12] This provided for a regime of prior approval, called the 'discharge consent regime', on which today's regulatory law rests. The idea behind the discharge consent regime was steadily to clean up the most polluted rivers and estuaries by preventing new discharges, or managing their impact on ambient quality through discharge consent conditions.[13] This is the system the Ashby Report had in mind when describing the British way as 'each case on its merits'.[14] Discharge permits (consents) were in practice granted in fairly standardised terms,

---

[9] On the adequacy of the protection of watercourses through the common law, where riparian proprietors had the means and volition to sue, see Second Report of the Royal Sanitary Commission, PP XXXV (1871) 22; and B Pontin, *Nuisance Law and Environmental Protection: A Study of Injunctions in Practice* (Lawtext Publishing 2013) 38–39.

[10] *Essay and Handbook*, n 3, 39.

[11] Bill Howarth comments that '[a]lthough well intentioned, the legislation of this period sought to legislate away water pollution by proclamation and little else'. W Howarth, *Water Pollution Law* (Shaw and Sons 1987) 1.

[12] In Scotland it was replaced by the Rivers (Prevention of Pollution) (Scotland) Act 1951. Northern Ireland did not have specific water pollution-relevant legislation until the Water Act (Northern Ireland) 1972.

[13] Section 7(1)(a). This was based on of the regulatory model advocated by the Pollution Sub-Committee of the Central Water Advisory Committee under the Chair of SJ Hobday in its report of 1949 (see Ministry of Health, *Rivers Pollution Prevention, Report of the Sub-Committee of the Central Advisory Water Committee* (HMSO 1949), hereinafter 'Hobday Report'). The estuaries covered by the Act which are listed in the schedule number 95. The Water Resources Act 1963 empowered river authorities to take samples from sea waters, but fuller regulatory law provision awaited the Control of Pollution Act (COPA) 1974 (s 31).

[14] Ashby Report, n 2, 58–62.

as regulators developed informal rules of thumb that enabled decisions to be made efficiently and consistently. For example, in the area of sewage disposal, a discharge consent would usually specify the '30/20 standard' (up to 30mg/l of suspended solids and a biochemical demand (BOD) of no more than 20mg/l).[15] Standardisation was a little harder with trade effluent beyond sewage undertakings, because of differences in effluent from trade to trade. Nevertheless, the 30/20 standard usually applied here, in addition to a control on the temperature of the effluent (no more than 30°C), and heavy metals of no more than 1 part per million.[16]

A particularly salient provision of the Act to flag up for elaboration later in the context of the controversial development of early Community law is section 5. This enabled the regulator to make bye-laws specifying river quality objectives to which consented emissions would have to conform. However, few bye-laws were proposed for ministerial approval, and *none* was approved. In announcing the repeal of section 5,[17] Viscount Simon said that the idea of fixed, formal limit values for discharges to water bodies was mistaken because it lacked necessary flexibility:

> [T]he effect of any particular source of pollution on a river does not depend solely upon the quality and the quantity of the effluent but also upon the condition of the water in the river at the point where it receives the effluent and upon the rate of flow of the river ... [W]e have to remember that organic pollution is naturally disposed of in all rivers and streams by the process of oxidation so long as there still remains a sufficient quantity of absorbed oxygen in the water; and even inorganic poisons are obviously less harmful the smaller the concentration in the water. So that the effect of any given pollution depends partly on what is already there in the water.[18]

Newsom and Sherratt had this to say about the absurdity of fixed limit values for prescribed substances discharged to watercourses: 'Whilst no doubt it would be possible to produce a list of specific poisons, the harmfulness ... of these depends on dilution.'[19]

Nigel Haigh has argued that Britain misled itself and the European Commission when it suggested that the British way was to set standards

---

[15] See Royal Commission on Sewage Disposal, *Standards and Tests for Sewage and Sewage Effluents Discharging into Rivers and Streams*, 8th Report, Cm 6464 (HMSO 1912).
[16] Ashby Report, n 2, 60.
[17] Under the River (Prevention of Pollution) Act 1961 and Rivers (Prevention of Pollution) (Scotland) Act 1965.
[18] HL Deb 3 July 1961, vol 232, cols 1177–94. For a detailed discussion of this issue, including the repeal of s 5, see *Essay and Handbook*, n 3, 43.
[19] J Newsom and JG Sherratt, *Water Pollution* (Sherratt 1972) 66 ('The quality and quantity of the dilutant is the crux and this varies from place to place').

for ambient river quality and leave emissions to be tailored according to them – an argument that was used to resist Commission proposals for an outright prohibition on the discharge of dangerous substances.[20] The repeal of section 5 demonstrated that it rejected ambient standards.[21] Yet the picture is complicated by 'soft law' (ministerial circulars) and inspection practice on the ground.[22] This suggest that regulators *did* work to an ambient river quality objective, albeit a flexible, qualitative one, namely, 'wholesomeness'. That was derived from the long title of the 1951 statute ('an Act to maintain and restore the wholesomeness of watercourses'). Though wholesomeness was not a statutory duty, it was the criterion to which the Ministry of Housing and Local Government had regard. Crucially, regulators 'may neither exercise nor refrain from exercising their powers ... in such a way as to permit any river to become materially less wholesome'.[23]

The meaning of 'wholesomeness' was informed by the classification of waters of England and Wales into the four classes with which this chapter began. As Keith Hawkins explains in his study of rivers pollution in the mid-to late 1970s,[24] regulators tended to prohibit discharges into unpolluted rivers, and subject to tight conditions discharges into class 2 (mildly polluted) rivers. In polluted waters the discharges would be subject to more generic conditions that, over time, could improve quality, turning grossly polluted water bodies into polluted ones, whilst accommodating economic considerations. Though not quite an 'each case on its merits' regime, the regulatory law at hand was pragmatic, and geared around broad qualitative notions of 'wholesomeness' and 'pollution', monitored by inspectors entrusted with wide discretion.

B. Common Law and Regulation: Private and Public 'Ordering'

This leads on to common law standards, and their contribution to the law of watercourses operating alongside regulatory law. The relevant black letter law was expounded by Lord Macnaughten in the Scots

[20] *Essay and Handbook*, n 3, 43–45.
[21] ibid 44.
[22] MHLG Circular 64/68, 4 December 1968. For fieldwork, see K Hawkins, *Environment and Enforcement: Regulation and the Social Definition of Pollution* (Oxford University Press 1984) esp 117 (on the stigma attached to pollution of rural rivers, where 'the local paper will go to town').
[23] Circular 64/68. Above n 22.
[24] Hawkins, n 22.

case of *John Young v Bankier Distillery*:[25] the common law entitles the owner of the banks of the watercourse to the water in its 'natural flow, without sensible diminution or increase and without sensible alteration in its character or quality'. Pollution is an 'invasion of this right', which is actionable on proof of damage (eg fish kill or eutrophication).[26] Following on from the comments at the start of this section, in Victorian times, enforcement of riparian rights by the 'country set' resulted in eye-watering sums being spent on pioneering treatment techniques and technologies for the protection of private property in water.[27] The investment in protecting private interests in water bodies has been criticised as disproportionate.[28] However, it has been defended, first, as an example of judges playing a constructive part in environmental protection[29] and, second, as reflective of the 'real costs' of rivers pollution.[30]

The politically delicate nature of the protection of water bodies by means of the enforcement of private rights surfaced in the immediate post-war era with the unreported action in *Brocket v Luton Corporation*.[31] The defendant was the statutory sewage undertaking for a population of 100,000 (up from 30,000 at the turn of the century). The plaintiff was the patrician Lord Brocket of Brocket Hall. To cater for growth in demand for its services, the authority, in the late 1930s, obtained approval for a sewage works (costing £450,000) discharging into the River Lee. When completed, in 1941, the works discharged sewage effluent that was heavily polluting of the river as it bisected the grounds of Brocket Hall. Once blessed with abundant fauna and flora, the river was 'now devoid of fish, insects and plantlife', complained Lord Brocket.

The defence did not deny the injury but emphasised the costs (an additional £100,000) of preventing it. The suggestion was that compliance with an injunction would entail more expenditure than the fish

---

[25] *John Young v Bankier Distillery* [1893] AC 691. For a fuller overview of current law, see B Howarth and S Jackson, *Wisdom's Law of Watercourses*, 6th edn (Sweet & Maxwell 2011) 71–81.

[26] *John Young v Bankier Distillery*, n 25, 698.

[27] Pontin, n 9; L Rosenthal, *The Rivers Pollution Dilemma in Victorian England* (Ashgate 2014).

[28] Rosenthal, n 27; S Tromans, 'Prevention or Payment (1982) 41 *Cambridge Law Journal* 87.

[29] Lord Carnwath, 'Judges and the Common Laws of the Environment' (2014) 26 *Journal of Environmental Law* 177, 178–79.

[30] Pontin, n 9.

[31] *Brocket v Luton Corporation* (High Court, 30 July 1948), before Vaisey J. A transcript is provided in Newsom and Sherratt, n 19, 191.

were worth. Further, the Corporation relied on the fact that the sewage works had been built to treat sewage so as to satisfy the regulator's (Lee Conservancy's) presumptive 30/20 standard. The problem was the volume of the effluent in relation to the size and flow of the river into which it was discharged.

One aspect of the case that highlights the importance of private law operating alongside the criminal-administrative regulatory law is Vaisey J's criticism of Lee Conservancy, the statutory regulator, for approving a works and/or taking no action to tighten the presumptive emission limit once the scale of the pollution became apparent.[32] This suggests that the common law fills gaps in regulatory law or poor judgment (from a pollution perspective) in its enforcement. However, the definition of actionable pollution is in 'common sense' or 'sensory' terms, which appears to complement the qualitative character of the objectives of regulatory law (rivers that are 'wholesome', 'unpolluted' etc). Thus the judge was not concerned with statistics about BOD but more with how the river looked (and smelled):

> I am quite satisfied that any person with eyes and a nose would have been certain in his own mind that here is a dirty river, a river of foul water, with an unpleasant smell, frothy and unclean, containing a large quantity of what I call sludge.[33]

A third aspect is the primacy attached to the riparian right to purity relative to economic considerations. The judge said that the court would not listen to the defendant's argument that the public interest in the river as a sewer was more valuable than as a private fishery: 'the cost is not really a material consideration to me – no public body is entitled to pour noxious solids and liquid into streams … which do not belong to it'.[34]

The sewage works, then, was injuncted, but the proceedings did not end there The injunction was suspended for 1 year and 11 months to allow for the raising and spending of £100,000 to treat the sewage more fully. A further suspension was later granted, to give the sewage undertaking the time it needed to complete the necessary improvements.[35]

What did the Labour Government make of this scheme of private ordering orchestrated by a member of the landed elite? It had set up the Hobday Committee to inquire into possible reforms of

---

[32] ibid 196 ('I must confess that I am rather surprised by the supine and complacent attitude' of [Lee Conservators]').
[33] ibid 192.
[34] ibid 197.
[35] G Armer, 'River Pollution Bill', 9 September 1950 (National Archive HLG 29/347).

regulatory law, and its relationship with the common law protection of private interests.[36] One objection to the continuation of common law protection was that the standard of purity was too strict for modern society, more reliant than ever on industry. Another was that its operation was unpredictable and even capricious; its enforcement depended on victims having the means and inclination to take action. This was a scarcely veiled comment on the elitism of the common law in practice (exemplified by the defence of Brocket Hall, 'where Lord Melbourne lived and Lord Palmerston died').[37] Yet the politics of private interests in water bodies was changing, in ways that made it difficult for a Government of the left to weaken the common law in this field. Working-class anglers had organised themselves into a litigation union, called the Anglers Cooperative Association (ACA), which leased rights from patrician riparian proprietors so as to confer standing in nuisance proceedings.[38]

Within a year of its inception, the ACA had initiated 'a number of cases' in respect of mostly coarse fisheries under threat from sewage and trade effluent.[39] The civil servant in charge of drafting the 1951 Act (George Armer) took the view that the Hobday Committee recommendation for a saving of common law needed to be revisited:

> It seems quite unreasonable that a private individual should be able to hold a local authority and its ratepayers to ransome [*sic*] to this extent. If Lord Brocket can do so there is nothing to prevent other riparian owners all over the country following suit, with serious consequences to local authorities and industry. An Anglers' Co-Operative Association has been formed recently, apparently with the main object of backing actions of this kind.[40]

Armer favoured a complete abolition of riparian rights to purity, and replacement by regulatory law. He drew an extended analogy with the nationalisation of the right to develop land under the Town and County Planning 1947.[41]

---

[36] Hobday Report, above n 13.

[37] Above n 31.

[38] For a history of this organisation, see R Bate, 'Saving Our Streams: The Role of the Anglers Conservation Association in Protecting English and Welsh Rivers' (2003) 14 *Fordham Environmental Law Journal* 375. After various name changes, this unincorporated association is now known as Fish Legal. It is under the umbrella of the Angling Trust.

[39] National Archives HLG 29/349.

[40] Armer, n 35, 2.

[41] ibid 2–3: 'Although one hesitates to suggest interference with common law rights it seems that there are overwhelming arguments in favour of doing so in this instance. Relatively few people would be affected and the loss of rights involved would be insignificant

Yet it was not easy for the Bill's ministerial sponsors – initially Nye Bevan and then Hugh Dalton – to share Armer's stance. The ACA's campaign of acquiring property rights in coarse fishing was perceived by them as an inspirational exercise in working-class self-help. The preservation of the common law in the face of 'regulatory taking' had the support of the influential working-class newspapers the *Daily Mirror* and *The People*.[42] The maintenance of the status quo also suited regulators, because nuisance law provided an 'unofficial' outlet for voluntary efforts to control rivers pollution – or more bluntly, it was a way of keeping rivers clean without regulatory intervention.[43] The final factors in favour of the anglers were the undertaking to the Minister by the ACA made an undertaking to show restraint in 'prosecuting' riparian rights,[44] whilst the Government received legal advice to the effect that courts would not permit anglers to stand on extreme rights.[45] The 'takings' clause was dropped after a long struggle, which took on constitutional proportions.[46] In its places was the nuisance savings provision (section 11(6)).

Encouraged by this victory, the ACA helped claimants bring 34 successful actions against industrial and town drainage undertakings in the 1950s and 1960s, covering hundreds of miles of rivers.[47] One case of particular importance both in its shaping of the law and its environmental impact, in cleaning up a polluted river, is *Pride of Derby* case,[48]

---

compared to many others which have occurred in recent years, for example, restriction on development under planning legislation ... It seems to me that we should be justified in abolishing the common law right of action entirely in the Bill. It might be possible to retain it in modified form with certain safeguards, but it would be difficult to do this satisfactorily and I think it would be better to start with a clean sweep and to keep this as a second string to our bow if we should be forced to retreat.'

[42] Anon, 'Gaol for Polluters in River Pollution Bill but Anglers may be Hit by Snags', *Daily Mirror* (17 November 1950); R Clark, 'The Scandal of Our Rivers', *The People* (7 January 1951).

[43] On lack of support among Rivers Boards for the common law 'takings clause', see HLG 29/348.

[44] Letter of 19 January 1951 from John Eastwood (ACA) to the Ministry (HLG 29/348).

[45] Advice Upjohn QC, 19 December 1950 (National Archives 29/347).

[46] B Pontin, 'Defending "Fundamental" Riparian Rights from Proposed Regulatory Law Limitations: Some Lessons from Parliamentary History' (2006) 17 *Journal of Water Law* 3. Industry lobbyists returned to the issue in the context of the Rivers (Prevention of Pollution) Act 1961, but officials advised the Minister (Lord Jellicoe) that 'there seems no prospect at all of removing this risk to polluters [of common law actions] after the abortive attempt to do so in the 1951 Bill' (Central Advisory Water Committee, 'Consideration of the Trade Effluent Sub Committee Report', para 13, National Archives, HLG 127/114).

[47] Newsom and Sherratt, n 19, v.

[48] *Earl of Harrington and Pride of Derby Angling Association v British Celanese and others* [1953] Ch 149.

brought by Lord Harrington (owner of Elvaston Castle) and the Pride of Derby Angling Club, to which Lord Harrington leased fishing rights in respect of eight miles of the River Derwent. The defendants were British Celanese Ltd and Derby Corporation. At first instance the plaintiffs were awarded an injunction by Harman J, restraining the defendants from 'causing or permitting any effluent to flow ... so as sensibly to alter ... the quality' of the watercourse. As with *Brocket*, the injunction was suspended, to allow the parties to work out a suitable fix.

The most convenient solution for British Celanese was to obtain the consent of the Corporation to discharge six million gallons of its effluent into the second defendant's sewers, passing the problem on to the Corporation.[49] The Corporation refused, because that would expose it to the risk of contempt of court proceedings in respect of the injunction. It could only accept the effluent if the injunction was lifted. It appealed the injunction, on the ground that it would require *unplanned* expenditure that would have to be authorised ministerially. What if authority was denied? This argument failed, because it became clear that the minister supported expansion of the sewage infrastructure.[50]

The case is most famous for Lord Denning's comment that 'the power of the courts to issue an injunction for nuisance has proved the best method so far devised of securing the cleanliness of our rivers'.[51] What happened in the aftermath of the case bears out Denning's perspective, as common law-shaped improvement in the Corporation's sewage infrastructure cleaned up this stretch of water over a period of 10–15 years.[52] But 'strong' private law protection against cleaning up pollution had an important unintended consequence for the development of regulatory law, namely, calls greater secrecy in the administration of the discharge consent regime. The 1958 river quality survey was never published, for fear that it could provide evidence that fuelled civil litigation in respect of stretches of water that were recorded as polluted. Furthermore, the application process for the discharge consent regime was reformed to

[49] M Lobban, 'Tort Law, Regulation and River Pollution: The Rivers Pollution Prevention Act and its Implementation, 1876–1951' in T Arvind and J Steele (eds), *Tort Law and the Legislature: Common Law, Statute and the Dynamics of Legal Change* (Hart Publishing 23) 351.

[50] The new works came into operation in 1958 (ibid 352).

[51] *Pride of Derby*, n 48, 192.

[52] The treatment works had a significant beneficial effect, such that by 1970 the river was fit for abstraction for drinking water. Ministry of Housing and Local Government, *Taken For Granted: Report of the Working Party on Sewage Disposal* (HMSO 1970) (Jeger Report).

prevent disclosure of details that could, again, provide evidence that was useful to litigious anglers. Parliament, in enacting the Rivers (Prevention of Pollution) Act 1961, took the drastic step of making disclosure of information relating to an application for a consent a criminal offence.[53] The offence carried a possible custodial sentence (unlike offences concerning rivers pollution at this time).

However, government policy on this point continued to evolve. Under the Control of Pollution Act 1974, the secrecy provisions of the 1961 Act were repealed and replaced with a system of public registers, publicising the terms on which discharges were consented and the records of compliance sampling.[54] A connection once again was made with developments in town planning, and in particular the increasing guidance offered by the principle of public participation in decision making espoused in the Skeffington Report.[55] The aim, as Burton explained in his review of operation of the registers, was to inspire 'public confidence' and 'positive goodwill'.[56] That was also the purpose of the *River Pollution Survey* of 1970, published in two volumes in 1971 and 1972. It contained colour-coded maps at a detailed scale (1:250,000), that made it possible to identify the class of a specific stretch of river.[57]

C. River Basin Management

So far mention has been made of 'the regulator' in loose terms, with occasional mention of River Boards (as regulators). Now is the place to address changes in the administration of the law over the period. In Victorian times, the locus of river pollution regulation was radically local. It was entrusted to local sanitary authorities, of which there were over a thousand in England and Wales alone. The Royal Commission on Sanitation reflected Victorian-era 'localism' thus: 'The principle of local government has been recognised as the essence of our national vigour. Local administration under central superintendence is the distinguishing feature of our government.'[58]

---

[53] Rivers (Prevention of Pollution) Act 1961, s 12(1) and (2).

[54] COPA 1974, s 41.

[55] *People and Planning: Report of the Committee on Public Participation in Planning* (HMSO 1969) (Skeffington Report).

[56] T Burton, 'Access to Environmental Information: The UK Experience of Water Registers' (1989) 1 *Journal of Environmental Law* 192, 208.

[57] *River Pollution Survey 1970*, n 1.

[58] *First Report of the Royal Sanitary Commission*, Parliamentary Papers XXXII (HMSO 1868) (quoted in *Essay and Handbook*, n 3, 10).

Localism conflicted with developments in the science of hydrology which appeared to support larger-scale administration. Shortly after the Rivers Pollution Prevention Act 1876, with its myriad enforcers, Frederick Toplis proposed: 'That the country should be mapped out into water-shed districts, each containing one or more complete river basin, and that a body of commissioners should be appointed to each district.'[59] He specifically proposed 12 River Basin Commissions for England and Wales, with extensive responsibility: 'Every drop of water falling in their district should be more or less under their control, from the time it falls on the land until it reaches the sea.'[60]

Bills were put before Parliament by the Duke of Richmond who took up this cause, beginning with the Rivers Conservancy Bill in 1878.[61] The Bill failed, but in the early 1890s three clusters of local sanitary authorities covering the Thames, Lee and Yorkshire and Ribble river basins amalgamated into river basin agencies, called conservators, whose powers were put into statute (making them statutory river basin conservators).

During the Second World War, the Milne Committee was appointed, to inquire into the case for an extension of the principle of integrated basin or catchment management. Its Report recommended the creation of 32 River Boards in place of the local sanitary authorities.[62] This was implemented by Parliament through the River Boards Act 1948. Thirty two River Boards became 27 River Authorities through further consolidation under the Water Resources Act 1963. The upshot of this river basin-wide regulation of water recourses in respect of pollution was that a third of the rivers of England and Wales were regulated by five large River Authorities: Yorkshire (3,556 miles) Northumbria (1,817 miles) Trent (1,511 miles), Thames (1,444 miles) and Cornwall (1,232 miles). These then were amalgamated into 10 Regional Water Authorities under the Water Act 1973. The commentator Elizabeth Porter expressed the hope that this new system would provide a 'complete' solution to public-interest water needs, whilst being 'flexible enough to respond to ever changing challenges'.[63]

---

[59] F Toplis, *Better Late than Never*, Society for the Encouragement Arts, Manufactures and Commerce, Report of Proceedings on the Conference on Water Supply, 16 May 1879. See https://archive.org/stream/annualconferenc00artsgoog/annualconferenc00artsgoog_djvu.txt.

[60] ibid 14.

[61] River Conservancy Bill 1878–1879.

[62] Ministry of Health, *Report of the Central Advisory Water Committee, River Boards*, 3rd Report, Cm 6465 (HMSO 1943).

[63] E Porter, *Water Management in England and Wales* (Cambridge University Press 1978) 3.

D. Performance in Practice

As mentioned at the outset of the chapter, river quality improved during the period leading up to Britain's entering the European Community.[64] More specifically, between 1958 and 1970 the percentage of class 1 (unpolluted) rivers had increased to 76.2 per cent (up from 72.9 per cent).[65] That equated to 2,500 miles of previously mildly polluted rivers improving to the point that they capable of sustaining salmon and trout as well as a variety of coarse fish. Quality also improved at the lower end. For example, class 4 (grossly polluted) rivers declined to 4.3 per cent (compared to 6.4 per cent). This reflected a lift in the quality of 326 miles of rivers that had previously been unable to sustain any fish life. Further improvement was recorded in the *River Pollution Survey Update 1972*, such that on entry to the Community, 92 per cent of the rivers of England and Wales were able to sustain trout (a class 2 criterion).[66]

The *River Pollution Survey 1970* pointed to the correlation between the improvement in rivers and investment in sewage infrastructure, in seeking to explain the trend in river quality. Expenditure on sewage infrastructure (including sewage treatment) rose in real terms from £700,000 in 1945/46 to £109 million in 1968/69. It is unclear how much of this was invested in sewage treatment (as opposed to, say, outfalls), or whether the impetus in legal terms was largely the 1951 Act or the dozens of civil actions brought by the ACA and the patrician ranks. The biggest rises in sewage investment were during the Attlee administration (which ended in accounting period 1951/52 at £16.9 million), but the trend was steady. In all but one year (1954/55) investment increased. Looking ahead, Secretary of State for the Environment Peter Walker estimated that a further £610 million of investment specifically in sewage treatment infrastructure would be necessary 'to bring [sewage effluent] into line with 1980 standards that river authorities would expect to impose'.[67] He did not elaborate on what those standards were likely to be, except that they would be stricter.

---

[64] The river pollution surveys noted at the outset are confined to England and Wales. For an early independent report in Scotland, see HD Turing, *Third Report on Pollution* (British Field Sports Society 1949).

[65] *River Pollution Survey 1970*, vol 1, n 1, [1].

[66] *River Pollution Survey Update 1972* (n 1 above).

[67] Department of Environment, *River Pollution Survey 1970, Vol 2* (1[6]).

A leading civil servant in Peter Walker's department, Martin Holdgate, had this interesting point to make about Britain's priorities at this time vis-à-vis the Community it was days away from joining:

> The various Directorates in the DOE did not think it [EU membership] would make much difference to our environmental policy. For we still saw ourselves as among the world leaders. Had we not been the first country in Europe to have a major environment department, headed by a member of the Cabinet? Had we not played a leading role in a number of international actions? Did we not have the oldest laws and agencies for environmental protection in the whole of the EEC? ... Had we not been among the leaders of action to deal with marine pollution in the Oslo, London and Paris Conventions? The expectation was that we would carry on much as before ...[68]

The section following explores that expectation in light of the experience.

II. THE BRITISH WAY DURING EU MEMBERSHIP

European Community water law developed in the 1970s and 1980s more rapidly than in any other area of Community environmental law but, as commented on by Ludwig Kramer in his leading treatise,[69] what matters is enforcement, and this proved 'extraordinarily difficult'.[70] Most of the Community's membership failed to transpose into national law in timely fashion some of the Directives concerning water quality standards, viz those aimed at surface water intended for abstraction of drinking water, for drinking water itself, and surface water supporting fish, including a specific measure on shellfish. The Bathing Water Directive divided southern and northern Europe, with Britain and Germany treating it as a Mediterranean tourist industry-precipitated measure of little relevance to their own territories and a therefore curious field of competence for the European Commission to be asserting.[71]

---

[68] M Holdgate, *Penguins and Mandarins: The Memoirs of Martin Holdgate* (Memoir Club 2003) 202. The Paris Convention is a reference to the Convention for the Prevention of Pollution from Land Based Sources 1972. The London Convention is a reference to the International Convention on the Prevention of Marine Pollution by the Dumping of Wastes and Other Matter.

[69] *EEC Treaty and Environmental Protection*, above n 1.

[70] Ibid 4.

[71] Council Directive 76/160/EEC Concerning the Quality of Bathing Water [1976] OJ L31/1. Britain designated 27 bathing waters, Germany 94 (compared to 2,824 by France

However, these difficulties were overshadowed by those surrounding the Dangerous Substances in Water Directive 1976.[72] This required the Commission to identify List 1 dangerous substances, which would be subject to Community-wide emission limit values set by the Commission and implemented by Member States through a regulatory system of prior approval.[73] It is unsurprising that something as fluid as the water environment should present difficulties for the emerging project of harmonisation of laws. But Kramer added a further complication – for him the critical one – of Britain's principled critique of emerging Community jurisprudence in this field. Britain did not welcome *any* aspect of the emerging Community water acquis, which it consented to reluctantly. Crucially, it vetoed the Dangerous Substance in Water Directive in the form in which it originated:

> The view of the United Kingdom is that the decisive criterion for all substances is the extent to which they damage the environment. Consequently, all that is necessary is to set and monitor water quality objectives. This is contrasted with the view that particularly dangerous substances ... should be regulated by limit values.[74]

When Britain refused to accept the principle of maximum fixed emission limits for List 1 substances, the Commission proposed a compromise in which it or any other Member State could instead authorise discharges flexibly, with reference to ambient quality objectives.[75] The solution was deeply divisive, and it was deeply contradictory in terms of the aim of harmonisation in law: it permitted divergent Member State systems, in which the discharge of a given substance was absolutely prohibited or permitted subject to the quality of the receiving water.

The difficult legislative history of the Directive weakened the authority of the Commission and its nascent environmental policies among Member States. On the one hand, within Britain, it appeared to vindicate the concern of advocates of the British way in a more general environmental context that the field was too complex for the Commission to handle.

---

and 1,907 by Italy). See R Wurzel, *Environmental Policy-Making in Britain, Germany and the COMMUNITY* (Manchester University Press 2002) Table 8.1.

[72] Council Directive 76/464/EEC of 4 May 1976 on Pollution Caused by Certain Dangerous Substances Discharged into the Aquatic Environment of the Community [1976] OJ L129/23.

[73] Art 3.

[74] Kramer, *EEC Treaty and Environmental Protection*, above n 3, 6.

[75] Art 6 provides for a 'limit value method' and a 'quality objectives method'. The latter is subject to a five-year review by the Commission – a 'safeguard' not applicable to the limit value method to which most Member States were expected to adhere.

Membership of the Community would require constant vigilance lest further harmful proposals for ill-fitting regulatory laws emerge. On the other hand, within the Community, the Commission's acquiescence to British 'exceptionalism' had what Kramer portrays as a knock-on effect in terms of 'slow progress' in implementing law *throughout* the water acquis.[76] Frustration at the widespread ambivalence among members towards the water acquis prompted the Commission to take proceedings against all 12 Member States for breach of the Dangerous Substances in Water Directive. That risked uniting Member States *against* the body whose job it was to safeguard the Treaty.

Nigel Haigh attributes the difficulty with the Dangerous Substances in Water Directive to the extent to which it was driven by the concerns of only a selection of members; it was, he suggests, addressed to 'problems of the Rhine, a river that drains one of the world's most heavily industrialised areas while at the same time providing drinking water for a large population'.[77] It did not speak to the interests of Britain, with its relatively self-contained hydrology and deep heritage of regulation and law. This, then, is an alternative appraisal to one which portrays Britain as priorising the economy and showing indifference to environmental concerns.[78]

The attraction of Haigh's analysis is that it acknowledges the significance of Britain's maritime boundaries, which constitute a basic physical condition for the evolution of a nationally specific regulatory system, compared to the necessarily more international (if not supranational) regulatory system which evolved in respect of the Rhine countries. This may account for the early development of river basin management in Britain, with its relatively high degree of control of river basins.

The hydro-politics of Britain may also account for other distinctive features of regulatory law and its wider legal context described above. For example, it is difficult to imagine how an approach to standards emphasising wholesomeness (as in Britain) could be attractive in circumstances (prevailing on the continent) where river basins are shared by numerous states and it would fall to different national courts (up and down stream) to interpret the meaning of 'wholesome'. In these circumstances the Commission's concern with what goes into rivers – and to

---

[76] Kramer, n 3, 4–5.
[77] N Haigh, *EU Environmental Policy: Its Journey to the Centre Stage* (Routledge 2016) 58.
[78] eg Wurzel, n 71, as discussed in ch 2.

look at this in quantitative terms – seems more attractive. To reiterate, accommodating each proved initially extremely troublesome for the Commission.

Whilst the 1976 Directive thus illustrates the British way as a shield, the subsequent development of Community law illustrates a more proactive, consensus-building role. Britain's negotiators teamed up with France in the late 1980s to urge the Commission to rethink Community water policy and law around river basin management lines.[79] Like Britain, but to a lesser extent (because of the complication of the number of its rivers that are international), France had river basin administrative structures for managing water resources by the early 1970s.[80] The two Member States cooperated to push for a Water Framework Directive that would consolidate various fragmented approaches among Member States into an integrated, hydrological system-based approach, focusing on ambient water quality measured in terms of a qualitative objective of 'good'. After a decade of negotiation, this initiative came to fruition with the agreement of the WFD.

To elaborate on the remarks made at the outset, Member States must establish river basin districts, defined inclusively (under Article 21(5)) as the area of land *and* sea, made up of one or more neighbouring river basins together with their associated groundwater and coastal waters. Article 13 requires a management plan to be produced for each river basin lying entirely within the Member State's territory, and for coordination between Member States where river basins are international.[81] It is through these plans that the Directive's objectives of good ecological and good chemical status are to be achieved – the deadline for which was originally 2015 but is now 2027. The public is to have formal opportunities to participate in the planning process.[82]

This is the regime from which Britain is exiting, with risks that are argued to be high.[83] Yet a number of points arising from the preceding

---

[79] A Jordan, *The Europeanization of British Environmental Policy* (Palgrave Macmillan 2002) 128. For further background, see W Howarth and D McGillivray, *Water Pollution and Water Quality Law* (Shaw and Sons 2001) 5.7.1–5.7.2.

[80] N Haigh, 'Environmental Quality Objectives in Britain: National Policy or Community Obligation', Working Paper (Institute of European Environmental Policy 1982) app 2, referring to Ministerial Circular, 29 July 1971.

[81] This applies to all of the Netherlands. See further C Suykens, 'EU Water Quantity Management in International River Basin Districts: Crystal Clear?' (2015) 24 *European Energy and Environmental Law Review* 134, 140. On the international law context of river basin management under the Directive, see M v Sijswick, 'EC Water Law in Transition: The Challenge of Integration' [2003] 3 *Yearbook of European Environmental Law* 249, 268–69.

[82] Art 14 WFD.

[83] Burns et al, *UK Environmental Policy Post-Brexit*, above n 7.

analysis give grounds for a more sanguine appraisal. One is that many of the fundamentals are modelled on the British approach. The idea of river basin administrative structures has already been mentioned, as has the provision made for public participation in discharge consent decision making under COPA.[84] Another British-shaped innovation is the switch from emphasis on point source emission limits to a focus on ambient river basin water quality, but here the crucial caveat arises. The definition of 'good status' owes little to Britain's way or style, including its pragmatism. It is, as Henrik Josefsson and Lace Baaner comment in their important critique, a political objective that is incoherent ecologically. There are various aspects of this critique to explore in relation to Britain's withdrawal from the WFD regime.

One concerns the reference point for good ecological status, which is a pristine environment. Water is of good ecological status if it has limited signs of anthropogenic interference. Pace Josefsson and Baaner:[85]

> The ambition of establishing reference conditions based on pristine states is controversial, because of the substantial difficulty in identifying such conditions, and because many variables in most river basins are fundamentally changed, owing to climate change, invasive species and changes in landscape, when compared to historic states. Furthermore, in a river basin, most ecological variables vary naturally, that is, landscape diversity, growth conditions and nutrient fluxes change in response to the evolution of channel morphology, hydrological connectivity, species colonization, human activity. Thus, the ecological status of a body of water is based on a continually changing combination of factors. This ecological understanding seems to be poorly accounted for in the Directive's objectives.[86]

This is a significant opportunity for improvement once Britain leaves the EU and its WFD.

A related weakness with the definition concerns the 'one out – all out' principle under Annex V, paragraph 1.4.2. According to this, a stretch of river will not be of good quality status if one quality element fails to meet the criterion – or put differently, the classification of a watercourse is determined by its poorest-performing parameter.[87] The idea is to prevent a stretch of water being considered compliant with the

---

[84] Above n 57.

[85] Art 2(21) and (22) and Annex V, paras 1.1. and 1.2.

[86] See Josefsson and Baaner, n 5, 467.

[87] See further the ruling on a preliminary reference to the ECJ on the meaning of Art 4 of the WFD in Case C-461/13 *Bund für Umwelt und Naturschutz Deutschland eV v Germany* [2015] ECR I-433.

objective when it is not *fully* compliant. The weakness in this approach is the mistaken ecological assumption that the quality of the ecosystem is determined by a single variable, when – qua system – it is quite the opposite.[88] Josefsson and Baaner recommend replacing the 'one out' principle with a more structural approach to quality.[89] Specifically, they recommend gearing quality around volume and flow.[90] This is the approach with which Britain entered the Community; and it is the thinking that underlay the repeal of section 5 of the 1951 Act.[91]

The result is that rivers are misclassified under the WFD. They are labelled as of poorer quality than 'structural' ecological health would suggest.[92] Applied to Britain, this explains why, in 2012, the Environment Agency reported that only 36 per cent of water in river basins was good quality, with no prospect of meeting the 100 per cent good quality standard by 2015. The domestic classification system touched on throughout earlier parts of this chapter gave a more rounded, broad ecological picture, and one that suggested ruder health than that of the WFD. The England and Wales system went through various iterations between 1958 (the original *River Pollution Survey* for England and Wales) and the General Quality Assessment (GQA) in operation between 1992 and 2008, but for each period most rivers are classified as effectively good enough.[93] The original approach had a rough and ready (partly intuitive) rule-of-thumb character. Though it was called a 'chemical survey', it was in practice mainly biological (focusing on fish-life), with a mix of aesthetics (is the river pleasing to the eye and nose?). This seems to preempt the concerns of Josefsson and Baaner.

This is not to offer an uncritical, rose-tinted view of domestic regulation. Britain's domestic regime was poorly designed on entry to the Community in two respects: first, regarding financial arrangements, there was substantial underinvestment in sewage treatment; second, the regarding the poacher–gamekeeper approach to enforcement, this placed

---

[88] Josefsson and Baaner, n 5, 473.
[89] ibid 472.
[90] ibid 474–76.
[91] Above n 18 and associated text.
[92] Josefsson and Baaner, n 5, 472.
[93] National Rivers Authority, *The Quality of Rivers and Canals in England and Wales 1990–1992* (NRA 1994). This replaced the National Water Council method: National Water Council, *River Quality – the 1980 Survey and Future Outlook* (National Water Council 1981); DOE, *River Quality in England and Wales 1985* (HMSO 1986); National Rivers Authority, *The Quality of Rivers, Canals and Estuaries in England and Wales 1991* (NRA 1991).

trust in regional water authorities who were both a major source of pollution and the body entrusted with enforcing the principal river pollution offences.[94] These defects, together with unusually low rainfall, contributed to the first decline in river quality since records began, in the surveys of the 1980s.[95] It was not until 2008 that quality returned to that of Britain's entry level.[96] The creation of the National Rivers Authority in 1989 addressed the poacher–gamekeeper problem, whilst privatisation of the water industry was certainly an attempt – if controversial – to address the problem of underinvestment.[97]

There is not the space here to discuss in detail other aspects of the water *acquis*. The high-profile omissions are the Bathing Water Directives 1976 and 2000,[98] and the Urban Waste Water Directive.[99] Each has played a significant role in directing investment in tidal and coastal water sewage infrastructure, which the domestic prioritisation of inland watercourses has tended to marginalise.

The Bathing Water Directive figured prominently in the campaign for remaining in the EU on environmental grounds.[100] It is undeniable that the Directive and its enforcement by the Commission brought forward investment in sewage treatment infrastructure, with tangible improvement in coastal waters servicing Britain's major beaches. But this was money that could have been spent on other priorities defined through domestic decision-making channels. British public opinion was slow to define coastal pollution as a serious concern compared to inland watercourses. The Anti Coastal Pollution League (ACPL) did not have

---

[94] See S Bell, D McGillivray, O Perderen, E Lees and E Stokes, *Environmental Law*, 9th edn (Oxford University Press 2017) 619–20.

[95] In the 1990 survey, top-end quality is reported to have had declined from 75% in 1972 (where it remained until 1980) to 63%, attributable to lack of rainfall and associated poor volume of water. NRA, *Water Pollution Incidents in England and Wales 1990*, Water Quality Series No 7 (NRA 1992). That year there was a record number of recoded river pollution incidents (28,143), with the biggest growth in incidents occurring in the agricultural sector.

[96] In England, always under most pressure from pollution, 80% of rivers were classed as good chemical quality and 73% good biological quality. In Wales the figures are 95% and 88% respectively. Environment Agency, 'Historic River Quality', available at http://apps.environment-agency.gov.uk/wiyby/37811.aspx.

[97] Water Industry Act 1989. For background to privatisation, see D Kinnersley, *Troubled Water – Rivers, Politics and Pollution* (Hilary Shipman 1988). For a critique of privatisation, see S Gordon, *Down the Drain: Water, Pollution and Privatization* (Optima 1989).

[98] Above n 74; and European Parliament and Council Directive 2006/7 EC Concerning the Quality of Bathing Water [2006] OJ L64.

[99] Council Directive 91/271 Concerning Urban Waste Water Treatment [1991] OJ L135.

[100] J Vidal, 'Brexit Would Return Britain to Being the Dirty Man of Europe' *Guardian*, 3 February 2016 (invoking the spectre of a return to 'filthy beaches').

the membership, or the influence, of anglers' groups (notably the Field Sports Society and the ACA). It *did* succeed in drawing public attention to the fact that beaches in some holiday resorts were in a 'disgusting state',[101] but it did not make a persuasive case for this being a concern for Parliament at Westminster (or the wider European Community), as opposed to local politics.

The ACPL case was not helped by local initiatives that showed what was possible in localities which strongly cared about coastal bathing water quality. Bournemouth Council responded to concerns about coastal pollution in the late 1950s by deciding that it was worth investing £10–50 million in sewage treatment to make the coast pleasing for bathers.[102] The central Government, a little later, commissioned research into the health risks of exposure to sewage in coastal waters, on the understanding that it would act on a serious health risk, but that is not what was found.[103] Lack of a public health justification for national regulatory law remained the thinking when the Bathing Water Directive was agreed. There was support in Parliament for the British Government's vetoing the proposed Directive.[104] In the event, the Government acquiesced on the basis of a calculation that it would be allowed to develop coastal sewage treatment at its own pace. However, this is not how things worked out. The European Commission forced the pace through enforcement action.[105]

Similar considerations apply to the Urban Waste Water Directive 1991 (UWWD). The European Commission acknowledged that it was going to be a most expensive Directive to implement.[106] As with the Bathing

[101] eg HC Deb, Beaches (Pollution), 7 July 1960, vol 626, cols 712–73.

[102] The figures involved in coastal sewage treatment as understood in Government circles come from *Essay and Handbook*, n 3, 91.

[103] Medical Research Council, *Sewage Contamination of Bathing Beaches in England and Wales* (HMSO 1959).

[104] See, eg, House of Lords Select Committee on the European Communities, *Pollution of Sea and Freshwater for Bathing*, 13th Report, Session 1974–1975 (HMSO 1975); Baroness White, Motion, 'Water Pollution: EEC Report', HL Deb 13 October 1975, vol 364, cols 721–62. Baroness White spoke to the Select Committee report conclusion that 'there would be a very strong public reaction ... [to] the kind of expenditure suggested as necessary [which] could lead to a serious questioning of Community priorities' (ibid col 725). Lord Ashby spoke of the foundering of the Bathing Water Directive's aim of 'harmonisation' in a mood of 'conflict, controversy, acerbity and general ill-will' (ibid col 736).

[105] For a discussion of Commission enforcement action against Britain in 1988 and the 'u-turn' on bathing water investment in the changeover of British Environment Secretary from Nicholas Ridley to Chris Patten, see Wurzel, n 71, 214–19.

[106] It estimated, in its unpublished impact assessment on the proposed Directive, that it would cost in the region of €60–100bn to implement: L Kramer, *Focus on European Environmental Law* (Sweet & Maxwell 1997) 22.

Water Directive, the investment lacked the support of Parliament at Westminster. It continued to believe in a 'dilute and disperse' theory, by which Britain maximised the natural advantage of strong tides into which sewage works could discharge minimally treated sewage, for the water to 'do the rest'. This pragmatic approach had the approval of the Royal Commission on Environmental Pollution because it allowed investment to be prioritised elsewhere, including in the area of inland watercourses, which was important given that high quality was under threat. The Jeger Committee had, prior to Britain's joining the Community, recommended that sewage was a resource that the country could ill afford to discharge raw into tidal waters.[107] But resource conservation was not the avowed purpose of the Urban Waste Water Directive. It was to raise the standards of sewage treatment to reduce pollution of rivers, estuaries and coastal waters.

A practical illustration of the difficulty of the UWWD in this respect is the 'Thames Tunnel case'. This is a reference to Thames Water plc's construction, under the authority of various regulatory consents and at a cost of over £4 billion (to water ratepayers), of a holding sewer to stop periodic storm-water flowing into the Thames tideway.[108] The rationale for the development is to enable Britain to act on the ruling of the ECJ[109] that London is in breach of the Directive in circumstances when raw sewage is discharged into the watercourse during storms. The case is dividing the green movement. The Thames Tunnel Now Coalition, including the Royal Society for the Protection of Birds, considers the initiative 'progressive'.[110] Thamesbank, by contrast, favours a more gradual and less 'hard hat' heavily engineered solution in terms of green infrastructure (more trees on pavements and roof gardens to retain water), and the recognition that, very occasionally, some storm water from London's sewers will legitimately enter the Thames, subject to in situ remedial measures.[111] On a clean-break

---

[107] Above n 54.

[108] Thames Water 'London's Super Sewer', available at https://www.tideway.london/.

[109] Case No 301/10, *Commission v United Kingdom*, 18 October 2012.

[110] Thames Tunnel Now Coalition, available at http://www.thamestunnelnow.org/.

[111] See Thamesbank Blue Green Partnership, available at http://elflaw.org/all-project-list/thamesbank-to-challenge/; and 'Relevant Representations of Thamesbank', Inquiry into the Proposed Thames Water Utilities Limited (Thames Tideway Tunnel) Development Consent Order (PINS reference WW010001), available at https://infrastructure.planninginspectorate.gov.uk/wp-content/uploads/2013/05/Thamesbank_TTT_Relevant_Representations_FINAL.pdf.

Brexit, disputes of this kind will be defined and resolved through domestic institutions.

III. CONCLUSION

If Britain adheres to the objectives under the WFD for any length of time after leaving the EU, as the 'soft Brexit' position advocates, there is going to be a significant problem of compliance with retained EU law, for reasons already explained. Even in home nations – Wales and Scotland – with the cleanest rivers, these are a long way off the pristine-inspired objective of all water bodies being good quality under the WFD.[112] Whilst the creation of a nationwide new guardian of retained law, the referred to in the European Union (Withdrawal) Act 2018, is an attractive idea whatever ones view on the merits of Brexit, this will not address the fundamental problem with the retained WFD, namely, that the objective is insufficiently nuanced bio-ecologically for investment in compliance with it to be justified. Crucially, this engages the deep structural problem anticipated by critics of EU competence in the field of the environment – that of objectives shaped by short term politics rather than practical ecological considerations as discussed in chapter 2.

Yet it is not easy to move on from this position, because, as Chris Hilson points out, 'taking back control in this context means taking back control to adopt weaker standards'.[113] Any relaxation in the objective will be seen as a step on the slippery slope towards Britain's once again becoming Europe's dirty nation. Hilson also comments that EU law has the benefit of flexibility in so far as Member States can adopt higher standards, but that does not cater for situations where, as with the water acquis, the standards are (too) high. In black letter law terms, a change to the retained law along the lines I advocate could fall foul of the Withdrawal Agreement which, at the time of writing, contains Article 2 of Part Two of Annex 4: 'the [European] Union and the United Kingdom shall ensure that the level of environmental protection provided by law, regulations and practices is not reduced below the level provided by

---

[112] S Priestley, *Water Framework Directive: Achieving Good Status for Water Bodies*, House of Commons Briefing Paper, CBP 7246 (2015).

[113] C Hilson, 'The Impact of Brexit on the Environment: Exploring the Dynamics of a Complex Relationship' (2018) 7 *Journal of Transnational Environmental Law* 89, 110.

common standards applicable...at the end of the transition period'.[114] The challenge, then, is to think imaginatively about the scope for a return to the pre-WFD criterion of 'good status' as something that is progressive. To that end it is helpful to note Bill Howarth's point that the 'continuing topicality of certain features of the recent history of water pollution law takes them out of the sphere of history and into the realm of contemporary legal concern'.[115]

[114] Article 2 proceeds to mention 'protection and preservation of the aquatic environment' as an area to which this non-regression clause applies. For a more general discussion, see C Reid, 'Environmental Commitments in the Withdrawal Agreement', Brexit & Environment, Blog, 15 November 2018.

[115] B Howarth, *Water Quality Law* (Shaw and Sons 1987) 31–32.

5

Air Quality

THE ENVIRONMENT WHITE Paper of 1970 claimed that a tradesman in Chaucerian England was hanged for the offence of burning sea coal as fuel in the process of manufacture, contrary to a proclamation of Edward I in 1307.[1] The claim is unsubstantiated, but there can be no disputing that domestic criminal law was set strongly against fossil fuel pollution of urban air in medieval and early modern Britain.[2] It is also clear that, moving into the modern day, no prosecutions for offences were initiated when, in December 1952, thousands of lives were lost in the 'Great Smog in London'. Between the coming of the smog on Friday, 5 December and its lifting on Tuesday, 9 December, four lives in a thousand were lost in the worst-affected parishes of East Ham and Stepney; that was almost double the rate of the most serious cholera and typhoid epidemics of the 1860s and 1870s. According to Peter Thorsheim, the combination of fog and pollution produced the 'deadliest environmental catastrophe in modern British history. By the time it was over, at least four thousand people lay dead'.[3]

Thorsheim's study is a helpful starting point because it highlights the complex meanings urban air pollution can have, which make it such a challenging subject of environmental policy and law. Many Londoners saw smog as commonplace. London was called the 'Big Smoke' for a reason. Thorsheim quotes from the *British Medical Journal* description

---

[1] Her Majesty's Government, *The Protection of the Environment: The Fight Against Pollution*, Cm 4373 (HMSO 1970) 6. This is described as a 'popular notion' without textual foundation in P Brimblecombe, 'Attitudes and Responses Towards Air Pollution in Medieval England' (1976) 26 *Journal of the Air Pollution Control Association* 941, 944. For King Edward's smoke proclamation focused on London, see Calendar of Close Rolls, Ed 1 m6d.

[2] E Ashby and M Anderson, *The Politics of Clean Air* (Oxford University Press 1981) 1; Brimblecombe, n 1; P Brimblecombe, *The Big Smoke: A History of Air Pollution in London Since Medieval Times* (Methuen 1986); W Cavert, *The Smoke of London: Energy and Environment in the Early Modern City* (Cambridge University Press 2016).

[3] P Thorsheim, *Inventing Pollution: Coal, Smoke and Culture in Britain since 1800* (Ohio University Press 2006) 163.

of the death toll as 'spectacular'.[4] Yet it was widely shrugged off by the public in terms of the vicissitudes of life, notably, weather in the context of infirmity (many of the dead had pre-existing respiratory conditions). Some died in 'accidents' resulting from lack of visibility. Was the smog substantially connected with emissions from power stations in Battersea and Fulham?[5] Few households acknowledged their own contribution, through open domestic fires that were in fact the main cause. Besides, was smog really a problem, as opposed to being part of London's magical identity?[6]

Over the longer term, however, the Killer Smog did change thinking. 'What was initially seen as a natural disaster eventually came to be seen as a catastrophe that human beings had helped to create – and which they might also prevent from reoccurring.'[7] This chapter examines the evolution of the British way of air quality protection in the period leading to Britain's European Community entry, covering both regulatory law and common law.

In the risk assessment Friends of the Earth commissioned, air quality and its policy and law are seen as being at 'high risk' when Britain leaves the EU.[8] There is, so the argument goes, 'a correlation between the existence and extension of the EU's air quality laws and the reduction in the UK of levels of acidification, ground and high-level ozone, and air pollution'.[9] Problems remain, particularly in connection with nitrogen dioxide, the limit values for which under the 2008 Ambient Air Quality Directive[10] are being widely exceeded. But the solution lies, so the argument continues, with infringement proceedings being brought

---

[4] 'Deaths in the Fog' *British Medical Journal* (3 January 1953) 50 (cited ibid 165). Devra Davis puts the death toll at around 10,000 (D Davis, *When Smoke Ran Like Water* (Basic Books 2002)).

[5] 'Fog and Public Health', HL Deb 18 November 1953, vol 184, cols 364–93, especially col 379 (Lord Haden Guest), col 381–83 (Lord Listowell) and col 383 (Lord Sempill).

[6] P Hennessey, *Having it So Good: Britain in the Fifties* (Penguin 2007) 120. 'For my generation of Londoners it [the air] did have a certain pungent magic. We can still sniff the smell of sulphur dioxide that swirled through every street from late September to early April. And we have all the stories of walking to school with but 10 yards visible ahead and the cars and buses creeping by.' The *Daily Mail* played on the supernatural mood regarding the killer smog in a cartoon published in 1953 (reproduced in D Elsom, *Atmospheric Pollution: Causes, Effects, Control Problems* (Basil Blackwell 1987) 199).

[7] Thorsheim n 3, 172.

[8] C Burns, V Gravey and A Jordan, *UK Environmental Policy Post-Brexit: A Risk Assessment* (Friends of the Earth 2017) 7, 28.

[9] ibid 28.

[10] European Parliament and Council Directive 2008/50/EC on Ambient Air Quality and Cleaner Air for Europe [2008] OJ L152.

before the CJEU by the European Commission. The concern is that 'in the absence of EU pressure to meet standards, measure quality and provide transparent data ... the UK will revise current air quality laws' downwards.[11] I offer a positive analysis, emphasising the enduring efficacy of the British way of air quality management, cutting across both substantive law and its surrounding governance.

I. THE BRITISH WAY OF AIR QUALITY MANAGEMENT 1945–73

Keeping with the Killer Smog of 1952, some of the literature is critical of the Government's handling of the episode, as evidencing complacence and secrecy, and raising serious questions of trust in domestic politicians and legal processes. Devra Davis comments disapprovingly on the refusal of the Minister for Housing and Local Government, Harold Macmillan, to accept an offer of help from across the Atlantic, when US tobacco companies ventured to donate cloth masks;[12] Macmillan preferred 'Britain's own useless face masks',[13] 3 million of which were made available from pharmacies on demand. You 'can't blame my colleagues for the weather', Macmillan is reputed to have said, when asked what the Government was doing to avoid a repetition of the tragedy.[14] Davis notes a 'secret' Cabinet memorandum expressing exasperation at the fuss that was being made in some quarters: 'Today everybody expects the Government to solve every problem. It is a symptom of the welfare state ... We cannot do very much, but we can seem to be very busy – and that is half the battle nowadays.'[15]

[11] ibid.

[12] Davis, *When Smoke Ran Like Water*, n 4, 46.

[13] ibid.

[14] ibid 45. Macmillan had a number of weather-related disasters to contend with around this time, beginning with the collapse of the coastal town of Lynmouth during the night of 15–16 August 1952, the aftermath of which he likened to the battlefields of Ypres in 1915 (A Horne, *Harold Macmillan: The Official Biography* (Membury Press 1988) 346). Thirty-four people lost their lives, and hundreds were made homeless. The 'Great Flood' on 1 February 1953, with North Sea levels 18ft above average in some areas, claimed 307 lives in England and 19 in Scotland. Macmillan's diaries reveal him to have been relatively unmoved by the 'London fog'. The entry for 8 December reads, 'Cabinet meeting called for noon. This was sad, as I had intended to shoot at Birch Grove. Another lovely day in the country, with impenetrable fog in London' (P Catterrall (ed), *The Macmillan Diaries: The Cabinet Years, 1950–1957* (Macmillan 2003) 198). On country air quality, see the last paragraph of section I. A.

[15] National Archive Memo, 18 November 1953, quoted in M Hamer, 'Ministers Opposed Action on Smog' (1984) *New Scientist* (5 January 1984). The Memo was released to the public under the 30-year rule.

It is understandable that what is in effect a future Prime Minister's dismissal of the cause of urban clean air as 'green crap' seems outrageously poor judgement in the context of one of Europe's biggest modern environmental catastrophes, and that Macmillan was being opportunistic in later claiming credit for the legacy, namely, the Clean Air Act 1956.

Yet Macmillan's shifting position on the issue bears a more sympathetic assessment when situated in the context of contemporary public ambivalence towards the smog phenomenon. The British public strongly supported controls on industry, but resisted control over home life. The 1952 smog episode did not move Londoners towards relinquishing their cherished 'open, pokeable, companionable fire'.[16] The open hearth elicited a deep sense of attachment as a fulfilling aesthetic experience, pleasing to the ear, the eye, and to all the senses. Use of stoves in which flames were hidden, though less polluting, was perceived as unhomely, or 'European'.[17] Householders knew that their domestic fires were seriously polluting.[18] But they could not imagine life without them, and campaigners could not break through this cultural barrier secure more 'effective' to pollution abatement.

A self-styled pragmatist in relation to public policy,[19] Macmillan listened both to the householders concerned to protect an ancient liberty of the hearth, and to the case put by clean air modernisers within and outside government. He was broadly persuaded that the domestic hearth *was* a problem to which there *was* a practicable solution. Equally, the law must be largely consensual, he emphasised. Rather than rush through clean air legislation – the Labour Opposition would have supported

---

[16] Ashby and Anderson, n 2, 64 (quoting distinguished sanitary engineer Sir Frederick Bramwell: 'We are strong of the … opinion … that we must have an "open, pokeable, companionable fire"'). See too George Orwell, 'The Case for the Open Fire' *London Evening Standard* (8 December 1945) ('the first great virtue of the coal fire is that, because it only warms one end of the room, it forces people to group in a sociable way').

[17] Ashby and Anderson, n 2.

[18] See the winter air quality statistics in the Committee of Investigation of Atmospheric Pollution, *Fifteenth Report*, 1929 (HMSO 1930), which bear out what was obvious to the eye. Suspended solids (from coal emissions into the atmosphere) in rainwater for Victoria Street are recorded as $34ug/m^3$ (weekday), $27ug/m^3$ (Saturdays), $38ug/m^3$ (Sundays); for Westminster Bridge, the figures are $72ug/m^3$ (weekdays), $90ug/m^3$ (Saturdays), $63ug/m^3$ (Sundays). One of the most polluted days of the year was usually Christmas Day, and on that day in 1879 a smog confined Londoners to darkness at noon and probably took hundreds of lives. Ashby and Anderson, n 2, 56.

[19] H Macmillan, *The Middle Way* (Macmillan 1938).

immediate action – Macmillan appointed a Committee of Inquiry under the Chair of Sir High Beaver, to make recommendations for law reform.[20] Out of this eventually emerged the Clean Air Act 1956, sponsored by Macmillan's successor, Duncan Sandys.

A. Looking for the Law: Air Quality Monitoring, Fuel Rationing and National Parks – Labour's Clean Air Policy and Law

Turning attention to the immediate post-war context of the London smog and wider air pollution concerns, the Attlee administration had the necessary Parliamentary majority to robustly tackle urban air pollution from domestic sources. It did not do so, yet neither did it ignore the issue. As an immediate step, it brought under central government control the Committee for the Investigation of Atmospheric Pollution, established at the International Smoke Abatement Conference and Exhibition held in London in 1912.[21] This voluntary, subscription-funded national air quality monitoring network had a diverse private and public membership, principally led by the directors of the two national clean air societies, namely, the Coal Smoke Abatement Society[22] and Smoke Abatement League of Great Britain,[23] which were later merged.[24] Other members represented local authority clean air practitioners;[25] government meteorologists;[26] academics;[27] medical practitioners;[28] and industry.[29]

The purpose of the network was to provide information to help firmly identify the extent and the causes of urban air pollution, to feed

---

[20] Final Report of the Committee on Air Pollution, Cm 9322 (HMSO 1955) (Beaver Report).

[21] It was brought within the Department of Scientific and Industrial Research. See S Mosley, '"A Network of Trust": Measuring and Monitoring Air Pollution in British Cities, 1912–1960' (2009) 15 *Environment and History* 273.

[22] Dr HA Des Voeux (Treasurer) and JS Owens (Honourable Secretary).

[23] Ernst Simon.

[24] In 1958, to form the National Society for Clean Air. See Ashby and Anderson, n 2, 97.

[25] eg Baillie Smith, Convener the Air Purification Sub Committee of Glasgow Corporation.

[26] eg Napier Shaw, Director of the Meteorological Office.

[27] Professor Julius Cohen of Leeds University.

[28] SA Vasey FCS, editor of *The Lancet*.

[29] Cadbury of Bourneville joined in 1923. George Cadbury was a campaigner for clean air, so that his workers could enjoy 'sun, light and air'. See Mosley, n 21, 279.

into policy making and regulatory law.[30] The main focus of monitoring was smoke (ie particles) and sulphur dioxide.[31] Money was invested in developing instruments for reliably measuring this pollution, such as the standard deposit gauge – modelled on the rain gauge – which became British Standard 1747 for the measurement of atmospheric concentrations of sulphur dioxide in 1951.[32] The results of the monitoring confirmed the disproportionate contribution of domestic sources of air pollution, notwithstanding that less than one-fifth of coal was consumed domestically (four-fifths were consumed in industry). Smoke and sulphur dioxide from the London sites was on average 2.5 parts domestic and 1 part industry in source;[33] whilst in Glasgow, the contribution of domestic to industrial source was 3.59:1 on weekdays and 5.71:1 on weekends.[34] The weekday hourly peak of ambient pollution in most conurbations was 10am, when emissions from still-lit morning domestic fires (people rose for work at about 6am) met with those from recently-fired factory furnaces.[35] This was followed by a subordinate peak at 4–5pm, when evening meals were prepared for the return of the workforce.[36] On Sunday, these peaks were pushed back two hours.

Findings of this kind had a catalysing effect on local authority members, stimulating experimentation in smokeless fuel zoning. Manchester Corporation – working with other members of the network (notably Ernst Simon) – took steps to create a smokeless zone in 1936, but ran up against legal obstacles (it was advised that the Corporation's enabling legislation did not empower smoke control zoning).[37] The powers were acquired under a reformed enabling Act of 1946,[38] and by 1952, over 100 acres in the city centre were zoned for the exclusive use of smokeless fuel.[39] Salford followed suit in 1952 and Bolton

---

[30] The Committee's first annual report asserted that 'it is only in this way that the information can be effectively utilised as an index of present effort and a guide to future action': 'Report of the Committee for the Investigation of Atmospheric Pollution, April 1914–March 1915' *Lancet Supplement* (26 February 1916).

[31] eg Committee for the Investigation of Atmospheric Pollution, *The Investigation of Atmospheric Pollution, Twentieth Report 1934* (HMSO 1935) 13–15; and *Twenty Second Report 1936* (HMSO 1937) 5.

[32] Mosley, n 21, 283. The cost of running a monitoring station for a year was £1,000 (ibid 277).

[33] *Fifteenth Report*, n 18, 7.

[34] ibid.

[35] This is from the distillation of annual report of Simon Mosley, n 21, 290.

[36] ibid.

[37] J Longhurst and D Conlan, 'Changing Air Quality in the Greater Manchester Conurbation' (1970) 3 *Transactions on Ecology and the Environment* 349, 352.

[38] Manchester Corporation Act 1946, s 35(1).

[39] R Heys, 'The Clean Air Act 1956' (2012) 345 *British Medical Journal* e5751; Beaver Report, n 20. The effect of the zones was to substantially improve local air quality.

in 1954. A handful of other innovatory authorities created smoke-free zones around this time, including, earliest of all, Coventry.[40] Its zone, which came into force in 1948, was based on a local referendum in which 27,990 citizens voted in favour of a smokeless zone (with 11, 302 voting against).[41]

But the Committee was also a catalysing force at a central government level. It reported from 1945 to eight government departments, including those responsible for fuel, electrical power, housing, local government and trade. In a report on behalf of the Ministry of Fuel, the Committee recommended that the Government exempt from purchase tax stoves and grates within which solid fuels could be more efficiently burned than open hearths.[42] This is one of the world's first green tax initiatives. Moving from fuel to housing, the Committee recommended a programme of expensive – but in clean air terms beneficial – prefabricated council housing.[43]

To elaborate on the housing issue, Labour's post-war programme of prefabricated council houses helped break the cycle of home comforts associated with open fires. 'Prefabs' introduced people to *homely* central heating, through a stove/boiler that was tucked discretely away, burning coke or another *relatively* smokeless fuel. The public responded positively:

> At a time of upheaval and change each temporary bungalow managed to combine both traditional and futuristic qualities without compromising either. It was a cottage on its own plot but a cottage that contained the latest labour saving kitchen and a central heating system.[44]

Hundreds of thousands of these dwellings were constructed between 1946 and 1949. They 'proved' the concept of a smokeless household, without open fires, and with kitchen appliances powered by gas or electricity rather than coal.[45]

---

[40] Ashby and Anderson, n 2, 99.

[41] ibid.

[42] Ministry of Fuel and Power, Fuel and Power Advisory Council, *Domestic Fuel Policy*, Cm 6762 (HMSO 1946) (Simon Report). A million stoves were sold under tax exemptions by 1951 (Noel Baker, WA, HC Deb 9 April 1951, vol 486, col 643).

[43] On the importance of linking policies on housing and air quality issues, see the Beaver Report, n 20, [69]. On relevant Labour Government housing policy, see B Vale, *Prefabs: A History of the UK Temporary Housing Programme* (Spoon 1995).

[44] Vale, n 43, 173.

[45] In contrast, 98% of living rooms in 'conventional' houses had open fires, and 25% of kitchens had ranges powered by coal. B Clapp, *Environmental History of Britain* (Longman 1994) 18.

Labour's fuel rationing also played a part in air pollution control, although it is unclear that that was among its purposes. Under the Fuel and Lighting (Coal) Order 1941,[46] coal was limited to 20 hundredweight, except in the south east where the limit was 15 hundredweight. That was a 'fair share', it was reasoned, given the north/south climate differences, but both limits were set at rather a frugal level, so that domestic consumption was lower after the war than before (and air pollution was controlled at source).[47] The cleanest coal, notably anthracite, was never brought on ration, but that was more to do with its mining being largely confined to South Wales, in too small a quantity to justify rationing's administrative burdens.[48] Conversely, the link between fuel coming off ration and air quality became explicit when, just before the Killer Smog, the dirtiest coal became freely available for the first time in over a decade. Called 'nutty slack', this soft and sulphurous fuel was marketed for its cheapness, to compensate the consumer for its unpleasant appearance and possibly also its polluting propensity.[49] The MP Willie Hamilton considered that this relaxation in rationing may have been responsible for the London smog death toll.[50]

Policy and law in relation to the 'countryside' is a further oblique aspect of the Labour Government's contribution to clean air. Designated under Part I of the National Parks and Access to the Countryside Act in 1951, the Peak District National Park was the first of a number of designations for open air recreation chosen for its accessibility to residents of smoke-filled towns and cities. Upwards of 16 million people lived in the industrial towns and cities of Lancashire and Yorkshire either side of it, for whom it was no more than an hour's train ride away. This might seem like passing the buck, but this and other parks were popular, making them an ingenious response to the complex contemporary politics of air pollution. The Act gave the respiratory systems of many townsfolk respite.

---

[46] Fuel and Lighting (Coal) Order 1941 (SI 1941/1281).

[47] This caused problems during the 'Big Chill' of 1946/1947. D Kynaston, *Austerity Britain, 1945–1951* (Bloomsbury 2007) 189–200.

[48] I Griffiths, 'The New Welsh Anthracite Industry' (1962) 47 *Geography* 389.

[49] 'Nutty Slack off Ration' *The Times* (25 November 1952). See further Thorsheim, n 3, 162.

[50] 'Nutty Slack', HC Deb 2 February 1953, vol 510, col 1460–62, esp col 1461 (on the 'co-relation between the derationing of this nutty slack and the increase in fogs in the London area' (Willie Hamilton (MP Fife West)).

B. The Clean Air Acts 1956 and 1968

In accordance with the Beaver Committee's recommendations, the Clean Air Act 1956 outlawed emissions of 'black smoke' from residences,[51] and empowered local authorities throughout Britain to designate smoke-control areas, where only prescribed smokeless fuel could be burned.[52] To ease the financial burden of the transition away from the open fires to heating systems that were smokeless, local authorities were authorised to fund at least 70 per cent of a resident's costs of converting to prescribed fuel.[53] In recognition of the national interest in local clean air, the Act provided that 40 per cent of local authority subsidy was recoverable from central government.[54] As Dr Edith Summerskill (Labour MP) pointed out, this was a 'human touch', which recognised that most people were reluctant to move away from their open hearths.[55] Thus, the sponsoring Minister, Duncan Sandys, Minister for Housing and Local Government, did not exaggerate the importance of the measure in his summary of the proposal put before Parliament:

> These are far-reaching proposals. They involve a number of quite complex technical problems and entail the expenditure of considerable sums of money. In addition, they raise important issues of policy, which directly affect local authorities, industry and private individuals.[56]

A later reform, under the Clean Air Act 1968, significantly shifted the locus of control towards central government, by giving the Minister power to require local authorities that had not already done so to put before them proposals for smoke-control area designations and plans for air purification.[57] This is similar to the power by which local authorities at risk of exceeding EU limit values are compelled to take remedial action by the Secretary of State under the Environment Act 1995.

Looking at the wider environmental context, it is necessary to appreciate that the transition from open fires to smokeless domestic heating

---

[51] Clean Air Act 1956, s 1.
[52] ibid s 11.
[53] ibid s 12.
[54] ibid s 13.
[55] HC Deb, 3 November 1955, vol 545, col 1233 ('[T]he hon. Gentleman [Bill Deedes, sponsoring Minister] knows precisely what the British character is like and how traditional we are. I would not admit that the statement which he made about fireplaces, and what he extracted from this Bill, will encourage people to be willing to have their fireplaces changed. There should have been a more human approach').
[56] HC Deb, 25 January 1955, col 39.
[57] Clean Air Act 1968, s 8.

was never intended to reduce Britain's reliance on coal qua fossil fuel. Rather, it was aimed to make energy from fossil fuels cleaner (and safer) *locally*. The Act had the unintended consequence of displacing pollution by, first, adding impetus to the growth of electricity generating stations situated outside towns and cities, with tall chimneys following a dilute-and-disperse philosophy of air pollution control, and, second, directing business towards manufacturers of smokeless fuel products, such as the Coalite and Chemical Products Company founded by Thomas Parker (whose services to smoke abatement were recognised by the bestowing on him of the Smoke Abatement Society gold medal).[58] The paradox of smokeless fuels, then, was growth in demand for electric heaters of one kind or another – bar heaters, heaters with fans, storage heaters – which were pollution-free at point of use but not source, and smokeless fuels, like the Bolsover works of Parker, which have left a toxic legacy of land contamination.[59]

The displacement of pollution from households to factories created the political conditions for an increased competence for the Whitehall-based Alkali Inspectorate (or the Edinburgh-based Industrial Air Pollution Inspectorate). Local authorities did not have the resources to add new smoke-control responsibilities to the existing industrial pollution-control functions under the Public Health Acts. The Alkali Inspectorate stepped into the vacuum.[60] Responsible for the regulation of 872 scheduled works prior to the Clean Air Act 1956, this rose to responsibility for 2,160 works under the Alkali etc Works Regulation Order 1958.[61] Gasworks, smokeless fuel factories and power stations all now fell within the Alkali Act regime, and its key regulatory tool of bpm.

The Royal Commission on Environmental Pollution conducted an investigation of regulatory law in regard to air pollution, published in 1976. It broadly endorsed the British way for the reasons set out in

---

[58] 'Thomas Parker 1843–1915', European Route of Industrial Heritage, available at https://www.erih.net/how-it-started/stories-about-people-biographies/biography/show/Biografies/parker/.

[59] P Thorsheim, 'The Paradox of Smokeless Fuels: Gas, Coke and the Environment in Britain, 1813–1949' (2002) 8 *Environment and History* 381. 'Toxic Site to be Redeveloped' *Derbyshire Times* (17 May 2013).

[60] Ashby and Anderson, n 2, 122.

[61] The Scots counterpart, the Industrial Air Pollution Inspectorate, regulated 416 scheduled processes. See Royal Commission on Environmental Pollution (RCEP), 5th Report, *Air Pollution Control: An Integrated Approach*, Cm 6371 (HMSO 1976) [97]–[99]. When Britain joined the Community the number of scheduled processes regulated by the Alkali Inspectorate had grown to 3,159 (ibid [80]).

chapter 2: that it is flexible, and realistic, and that it makes appropriate use of the carrying capacity of the environment, so that money was
not wasted on pollution mitigation efforts that were unnecessary.[62] It
combined local control responsive to local politics with national control
benefiting from the world-leading expertise of Alkali Inspectorate. In
the spirit of the British way of incremental development, it was recommended that there was scope for further reform, notably through the
Alkali Inspectorate's setting of ambient air quality *guidelines*, for a
wider range of air pollutants.[63] This is returned to later, in section 2.

C. Common Law

The extent to which residents acquiesced in one another's polluting
hearths meant that the protection of private property, covered within the
parameters of nuisance, was not effective in tackling the causes of smog.
However, it has had a demonstrable impact in remedying industrial air
pollution. Medieval *Dalby v Berch*,[64] early modern *Jones v Powell*,[65]
industrial-era *Tipping v St Helen's Smelting*[66] and inter-war *Manchester
Corporation v Farnworth*,[67] all arose from polluting coal-fired trade
processes, which the court remedied by means of injunctions in the more
recent cases. Attention elsewhere has been given to a post-war case which
highlighted a new kind of plaintiff who sought the help of the common
law: *Halsey v Esso Petroleum*.[68] Thomas Halsey successfully sued the
owner of an oil storage depot opposite a terrace of residential houses,
in respect of the emission of acid particles, which interfered with the
plaintiff's property. He obtained an injunction, which, as usual, was
suspended to allow the defendant to organise its affairs (in this instance
eventually relocating to Fawley, in Hampshire).

What makes this a distinctively post-war development, relevant to my
British way argument, is that the action was funded out of the civil legal
aid budget established under the Legal Aid and Advice Act 1949. The aim

---

[62] ibid [182].

[63] ibid [175]–[176]. Among the pollutants suggested for guideline ambient air quality
values is nitrogen dioxide, which is the focus later in the chapter.

[64] *Dalby v Berch* (1330) YB Trin 4 Edw III, fo 36, pl 26; 4 Lib Ass 3.

[65] *Jones v Powell* (1629) 123 ER 1155.

[66] *Tipping v St Helen's Smelting* (1865) 11 HL Cas 642.

[67] *Manchester Corporation v Farnworth* [1930] AC 171.

[68] *Halsey v Esso Petroleum Ltd* (1961) 1 WLR 683. The discussion of the context of
this action draws upon B Pontin, *Nuisance Law and Environmental Protection* (Lawtext
Publishing 2013) ch 5.

of the was to 'ensure that all members of the community receive the legal assistance they require'.[69] Halsey lived in social housing. Without legal aid he would not have had any prospect of proceeding with the claim against one of the world's largest multinational oil companies. (His own legal costs alone were £25,000.) He was the '[g]rey haired van driver … who took on the might of a multi-million-pound oil company'[70] and won, thanks to central government-funding of civil litigation.

In fact, Mr Halsey was not quite alone, and this leads onto a further 'modern' aspect of the litigation. As well as public funding of the action, he enjoyed the moral support of 500 fellow members of the Riverside Community Association, which was formed in the late 1950s to pressure Fulham Council into limiting the growth of heavy industry in the area and/or better controlling pollution from industrial chimneys. This was a 'hidden' class action, rather than a rehearsal of an individualistic, or rather atomised, process geared around private property that sometimes characterises the enforcement of nuisance law.[71] Even so, there remained a gulf in economic wealth between the parties, on which the trial judge took the unusual step of commenting.[72]

The victory for the 'little man' raises important issues concerning the relationship between regulatory law and nuisance law. The timing of the litigation places it after the enactment of the Clean Air Act 1956. Why was none of the regulatory law so far described able to pre-empt the dispute? Witness testimony suggests that the Act had little impact in this neighbourhood. Violet, Halsey's wife, had spoken of 'oily partic-ulates coming out of the [Esso] chimney like black snow'.[73] Halsey complained of 'black smuts as big as half crowns'.[74] Fulham was one of London's first areas designated under the 1956 Act. Why was a civil action necessary?

The explanation given by the Council was that the defendant had a strong defence of using best practicable means (bpm) to avoid pollution,

---

[69] Her Majesty's Government, *Report of the Committee on Legal Aid and Legal Advice in England and Wales*, Cm 6641 (HMSO 1945) [126].

[70] '"Little Man" wins High Court Case', *West London Observer* (24 February 1961).

[71] On the tension between 'rugged individualism' and more collectivist thinking under-pinning nuisance law and its enforcement, see M Lunney, K Oliphant and D Nolan, *Tort Law: Text and Materials*, 6th edn (Oxford University Press 2017) 648ff.

[72] *Halsey*, n 68, 688.

[73] 'Firm is Sued in the High Court', *Fulham Chronicle* (10 February 1961), cited by Pontin, n 68, 140.

[74] Pontin, n 68, 140. For similar imagery in a similar period, see D Kynaston, *Smoke in the Valley: Austerity Britain 1948–1951* (Bloomsbury 2007) 109 (the air is described as polluted by 'the negative of snowflakes').

such that proceedings would have been a waste of time and money.[75]
I have mentioned above the economic constraints within which a local
authority operated in the field of local air quality management, and
the point to make here that the common law protection of property is
a valuable aspect of the broader picture of domestic environmental law.
Nuisance law in *Halsey* offered the people of Rainville Road an alternative to regulatory law, which did not rely on the means and volition of
local officers working within a regulatory regime that was particularly
sympathetic to the needs of industry (or so it seemed).

The above dynamics are not confined to local authority management
of air quality. The Alkali Inspectorate was often in a position similar to
that of Fulham Council, caught between victims of air pollution who
demanded tougher action and were frustrated by bpm, and perpetra-
tors who reminded them why cleaner processes should only be insisted
on when practicable.[76] An example with clear parallels to *Halsey* is the
dispute between residents of Port Tennant, Swansea, and the US-owned
United Carbon Black factory that polluted the air in the neighbourhood. Throughout the 1960s, residents within the neighbourhood
urged the works to abate acid smuts that interfered with their homes.
In January 1970, the protesters took the dispute to a more intense
level.[77] Dirty washing was dumped at the factory gate, with a demand
to immediately desist from emitting acid smuts into the atmosphere of
the neighbourhood.

What was initially a dispute between residents and factory took on
a different complexion when the Alkali Inspectorate was asked to intervene on behalf of the residents. The Inspector said that he was unable
to help. The factory's processes were complying with the statutory
requirement of bpm to abate pollution. Residents responded with tactics
of passive (and aggressive) resistance. They blockaded the factory for
24 days. Pollution-monitoring equipment belonging to Swansea Council

---

[75] 'Report to the Council on the High Court Action', Fulham Council Minutes
(24 March 1961).
[76] B Pontin, 'Tort Law and Victorian Government Growth: The Historiographical
Significance of Tort in the Shadow of Chemical Pollution and Factory Safety Regulation'
(1998) 18 *Oxford Journal of Legal Studies* 661; B Pontin, 'Nuisance Law, Regulation and
the Invention of Prototypical Pollution Abatement Technology: "Voluntarism" in Common
Law and Regulation' in R Brownsword, E Scotford and K Yeung (eds), *Oxford Handbook
of Law, Regulation and Technology* (Oxford University Press 2017) 1253, 1260ff.
[77] J Bugler, *Polluting Britain: A Report* (Penguin 1972); I Bone, 'Carbon Black' (1972) 6
Solidarity: For Workers' Power 1 (available at https://forworkerspower.wordpress.com/tag/
swansea/.)

was vandalised, as a token of frustration at the indifference of regulatory law and regulators. Yet, as in *Halsey*, the ultimate practical solution
lay with nuisance law. Though the protestors did not embark on formal
nuisance proceedings, the factory was advised, by in house lawyers, of its
common law obligation to respect residents' property rights. It agreed to
limit production when there was a strong easterly wind carrying pollution into neighbours' homes.

D. Air Quality Trends

Within the framework described above local air quality demonstrably
improved. In particular regard to the Clean Air Act 1956, millions of
pounds of grants were paid under the regime to residents in smoke-
control areas, to help them convert to smokeless fuels. In 1964/65 the
grant was £2.2 million, whilst in 1969/70 it was £5.1 million.[78] Though
this is a fraction of the public investment in sewage treatment to protect
rivers noted in chapter 4, it nevertheless had a substantial impact in
reducing suspended particles in the atmosphere (smoke). The *National
Survey of Air Pollution 1961–1971* disclosed that urban ground level
concentrations of smoke had fallen from 150μg m^3 in 1961 to 40μg m^3
in 1971.[79] 'There are places [in towns and cities] where so little coal is
burned that smoke is no problem', the Environment White Paper of 1970
asserted.[80] Stanley Johnson reflected enthusiastically on progress under
the Act: 'Whereas ... in 1952, 4,000 people died in the great London
disaster, 18 years later we were rather smug about smog.'[81]

The trend for sulphur dioxide was what Ashby and Anderson
consider 'less impressive'.[82] Urban ground level concentrations fell
from 150μg m^3 to 100μg m^3. The problem, once again, was the paradox of smokeless fuel. Overall emissions to the atmosphere rose from
3.9 million tons in 1939 to 6 million tons in 1968,[83] because of the

---

[78] Her Majesty's Government, *The Protection of the Environment: The Fight Against
Pollution*, Cm 4373 (HMSO 1970) [16]. To this should be added nationalised industry-
specific expenditure on bpm, notably £15.3m in 1968/69 by the electricity sector, and
£10.3m by iron and steel (ibid table 1).
[79] Department of Trade and Industry and Warren Springs Laboratory, *National Survey
of Air Pollution 1969–1971* (HMSO 1972).
[80] *The Protection of the Environment*, n 1, 8.
[81] S Johnson, *The Politics of the Environment: The British Experience* (Tom Stacey
1972) 172.
[82] Ashby and Anderson, n 2, 142.
[83] Clapp, n 45, table 3.1.

growth of power stations generating clean-at-point-of-use electricity, producing large qualities of unmitigated sulphur dioxide, dispersed over long distances by tall chimneys. In the Environment White Paper it was predicted (based on projections of the Clean Air Council) that sulphur dioxide emissions would fall only a little, to 5.5 million tons in 1975 and 5.16 million tons in 1985. Yet it did not reckon on the boost provided by North Sea gas. The switch to gas central heating and cooking led to steep reductions. At 3.7 million tons in 1986, sulphur dioxide emissions were the lowest since the 1930s.

As Britain entered the Community, it thus had in hand a source of pollution (particles) that had eluded control for many centuries. Through implementation of the Clean Air Act regime, the percentage of homes with an open fire fell from 98 per cent in 1945 to 20 per cent in 1975. Crucially, new challenges were emerging. The Warren Spring Laboratory, which had taken over monitoring from the Committee for Investigation of Atmospheric Pollution in the 1960s, had started to shift attention to future challenges, notably oxides of nitrogen caused by the increasing incidence of motor vehicles, in increasingly dense local concentrations.[84] The emergence of a 'car culture', or rather one built around the internal combustion engine, contributed to a narrative of normalising air pollution as strong as that operating in London in the days (years and centuries) leading up to the Killer Smog.

II. THE BRITISH WAY DURING EU MEMBERSHIP: ROADSIDE NITROGEN DIOXIDE REGULATION

This section examines Britain's experience of air quality management within the Ambient Air Quality Directive 2008 regime,[85] which addresses air pollution in the EU's towns and cities.[86] The original Ambient Air Quality Directive (1980) focused on smoke (particles) and sulphur dioxide.[87] It did so by setting limit values for these pollutants,

---

[84] RCEP, 5th Report, n 61, [304].

[85] At n 10.

[86] It requires Member States to designate and notify the European Commission of 'zones or agglomerations'. There are 43 in respect of Great Britain and Northern Ireland, and a further 1 in respect of Gibraltar: European Commission, 'UK Atlas of Air Quality Zones and Monitoring Stations 2013 and 2014', available at http://ec.europa.eu/environment/air/pdf/quality_by_country/UK_AirQualityZones_Current_opt.pdf.

[87] Council Directive 80/779/EEC [1980] OJ L229 on air quality limit values for sulphur dioxide and suspended particulates. For a comment on the slow development of the EU air acquis relative to waste, water and even nature conservation, see A Weale, 'Environmental

to be achieved by a deadline in the future (for particulate matter (PM) and sulphur dioxide (SO_2) that was 1993). Onto this template has been subsequently grafted further limit values relating to additional pollutants, including limit values for nitrogen dioxide (NO_2) – the focus of this section – under the 1999 Directive.[88] The limit value for NO_2 is derived from the World Health Organisation (WHO) guideline of an annual mean limit value for the gas of $40 \mu g \, NO_2/m^3$. The deadline for compliance was initially January 2010, but in the face of the prospect of widespread non-compliance (particularly within the Community's leading economies), this was extended to January 2015 under the 2008 Directive.

The argument for retaining EU law and broadly recreating its environmental governance system is based on the anxiety that politicians in an independent Britain will give in to vested economic interests, which will lobby for a relaxation in air quality standards. In regard to NO_2, the main cause of pollution is emissions from diesel and petrol vehicle exhausts, with the vested interests being everyone associated with the 'car industry' – a dauntingly big pool. There is no doubt that compliance with EU law is a struggle for Britain, as for others. The country started 2018 as one of 13 Member States against which the European Commission was proceeding in respect of this pollutant.[89] It was joined by four of the EU-6 (Belgium, France, Germany and Italy).[90] London's NO_2 emissions around the time of the 2016 Referendum were among the highest of any European city, at over $100 \, \mu g \, NO_2/m^3$. A staggering 93 per cent of UK zones or agglomerations were in breach in January 2010. How, in these circumstances, can leaving this regime be argued to be a positive development?

Rule Making in the EU' (1996) 3 *Journal of European Public Policy* 594. The British Government purported to implement the Directive within the framework of the Clean Air Act 1956, by completing the programme of clean air zoning in respect of coal-mining districts that had neither volunteered to zone nor been compelled to by the Government under the 1968 Act. See N Haigh, *EEC Environmental Policy and Britain: An Essay and Handbook* (ENDS 1984) (hereinafter '*Essay and Handbook*') 177. It also delayed the planned closure of monitoring stations that came into existence in Edwardian times through the 'network of trust', discussed at n 21 and associated text.

[88] Council Directive 1999/30/EC relating to limit values for sulphur dioxide, nitrogen dioxide and oxides of nitrogen, particulate matter and lead in ambient air [1999] OJ L163; European Parliament and Council Directive 2002/3/EC relating to ozone in ambient air [2002] OJ L67.

[89] European Commission, 'Press Release', 19 January 2018, available at http://europa.eu/rapid/press-release_IP-18-348_en.htm.

[90] ibid.

The starting point is the enormous complexity of local air pollution law for Britain as an EU Member State. The 'system' is characterised by two parallel national regimes. First, the *domestic* national regime, which operates through 389 local authorities, monitoring and assessing local air quality, identifying problem areas, and addressing them through action plan powers they are given by Parliament at Westminster. The regime is modelled on the Clean Air Acts 1956 and 1968, as modernised by the Environment Act 1995. It is national in the sense that the Clean Air Act was, that is, the competent central government minister has statutory powers to make directions to local authorities, and all actors work under the supervision of the courts by means of judicial review.

Second, the *EU-originating* national regime, under which Britain, for administrative purposes, is divided up into 44 zones (including the zone of Gibraltar).[91] This regime is subtly different at all levels from the domestic one. As well as the difference in the scale of its operation – the local administration is larger scale than the domestic-originating regime – the EU regime has different air quality modelling requirements, arrangements for exceedance reporting and action planning, and, crucially, differences in the legal status of exceedance. Commentators specialising in local air quality management talk of a 'gulf' between these national regimes.[92]

Before looking more closely at the enforcement of these regimes, it is important to acknowledge that the complexity is, bluntly, of Britain's making. One way of simplifying the job of local air pollution management would have been to move away from the pre-Community architecture when transposing the Ambient Air Quality Directive. That course of action would have entailed a fresh start – a clean break – embracing a regime built around Community-notified zones. That is the relatively simple approach that Member States unencumbered by a rich history of law and regulation in this field have adopted.[93] Alternatively, it could have vetoed the development of Community local air quality law on the grounds of unnecessary complexity. This would have had the support of the Royal Commission on Environmental Pollution, and Parliament at Westminster.

---

[91] See n 86.

[92] J Barnes et al, 'Policy Disconnect: A Critical Review of UK Air Quality Regulation in Relation to EU and LAQM Responsibilities over the last 20 Years' (2018) 85 *Environmental Science and Policy* 28.

[93] See generally L Kramer, *Focus on European Environmental Law*, 2nd edn (Sweet & Maxwell 1997) 5.

Based, as ever, on experience, the Royal Commission met with officials from the European Commission, advising that binding standards, with deadlines, would be 'unenforceable in practice and *would bring the law into disrepute*':[94]

> We do not think that air quality standards would be a sensible way of achieving [better air quality] ... We mean by standards, specified pollutant concentrations (however defined and measured) which the control system should not allow to be exceeded ... *We propose the establishment of air quality guidelines. These would not have legal force* ...[95]

The Royal Commission recommended guidelines that shadowed those of WHO. The Organisation had an air quality group in which 'network of trust' member Patrick Lawther was an active participant.[96] Its governance model, unlike that of the Community, was largely inter-governmental and, unlike that of the Community, global in application. The Royal Commission considered that a good model. This is broadly speaking the Clean Air Act–Environment Act model.

The Royal Commission recommended that the British Environment Minister (Denis Howell) use the need for consensus in early Community environmental decision making to secure a better-designed air quality regulatory law, if, that is, the Commission was to persist with its assertion of an unspoken Treaty mandate to intervene in this field. Howell acknowledged that 'the use of air quality standards to be achieved by a stated time represents a new departure for us'.[97] However, he pushed on with supporting Commission's proposals. He argued that the Directive was in Britain's interest, because: (i) there would be 'no legal penalties' for breach; (ii) 'it is left to us to determine how we must meet the required standard'; and (iii) Britain would find it easier than other Member States to comply because it had a head start through the Clean Air Act 1956, which (along with other aspects of the legal framework) would ensure formal and practical compliance.

A possible justification for Howell's stance is that it shows solidarity with the Community project in its infancy. This was particularly welcome within the Commission, at a time of discord in this and other environmental fields.[98] But that does not address the objection that the

---

[94] RCEP, 5th Report, n 61, [183] (emphasis added).

[95] Ibid [167]–[169] (emphasis added).

[96] 'Patrick Lawther: Obituary' (2008) 372 *The Lancet* 624.

[97] 'European Community (Atmospheric Pollution)', HC Deb 18 May 1977, vol 932, cols 601–20, col 603 (quoted in *Essay and Handbook*, n 87, 172).

[98] Not only in relation to water, discussed in ch 4, but in relation to air too. See the demise of the proposed Council Directive on the Sulphur Content of Fuel Oil (COM (75) 681), to which Britain objected in principle (see *Essay and Handbook*, n 87, 170).

formalisation into legally binding standards WHO guidelines would bring the law into disrepute because it would be extremely difficult to comply with and thus enforce. Howell seems indifferent to this objection, suggesting that the deadlines would be treated flexibly under the EU system.

In a press release commenting on the recent legal proceedings being considered against almost half the EU's Member States (and over half in respect of PM), Commissioner Karmenu Vella spoke of his frustration. Formal action, he said, was 'the end of a long, some would say too long, period of offers to help, advice given, and warnings made':[99]

> Our first responsibility as the Commission is to the millions of Europeans – young and old, sick and healthy – who suffer from poor air quality. Parents of a child suffering from bronchitis or a daughter of someone with pulmonary disease want to see improvements in air quality as soon as possible. For them, action plans with a 10–12 year timescale or ineffective plans are useless.

The reference to 'responsibility' for European health on the part of the Commission is thought-provoking. It highlights the transformation in the Commission's competence from one geared around freedom of movement of goods (subject to health-based barriers) to broader responsibility for 'EU citizens' health. Yet what is the nature of this responsibility?

'Responsibility' here means formal legal responsibility grounded in guardianship of the EU Treaty. In that name, at the time of writing, the Commission has whittled down the 13-strong list of Member States in breach of the NO_2 limit values to three, against which it is bringing infringement proceedings before the CJEU.[100] The three are Britain, Germany and France: Germany has the most zones for these purposes (26), followed by Britain (16) and France (12). What message is the Commission giving by proceeding against the EU's three largest economies? Is this a show of strength on the part of the Commission, that Member State wealth does bestow privilege or immunity? Or of weakness on the part of the Community as a whole, that the most successful, or at least the largest, economies have the gravest urban air quality problems?

One aspect of this to discuss in relation to advocacy in the literature of Commission-like governance is the length of time it has taken for

---

[99] European Commission, Press Release, 'Air Quality: European Commission Takes Action to Protect Citizens from Air Pollution' (17 May 2018), available at http://europa.eu/rapid/press-release_IP-18-3450_en.htm.
[100] Ibid.

the Commission to bring infringement proceedings, and the comparison in this respect between the proceedings with a domestic origin brought by ClientEarth and those brought by the Commission.[101] When *ClientEarth (No 1)* was brought in 2011, the British Government acknowledged that it was in breach of the 2008 Directive across the board, that is, in all 43 zones. ClientEarth subsequently pursued legal proceedings against Britain in respect of this admission on two fronts: national judicial review of the Government, seeking a declaration of breach and a mandatory order to remedy it; and a citizen complaint under the EU Treaty, alleging breach of EU law for the Commission to enforce. Though it was never intended as a race between EU and domestic governance channels for enforcing EU-derived obligations, the different pace of the parallel proceedings is nonetheless interesting.

Thus, it is unclear how long it will be before the European Court rules on the Commission's allegations. However, domestic litigation has unfolded rapidly. In the time between the Commission issuing a reasoned opinion (that Britain was in breach) in 2014, ClientEarth has won two further judicial review claims against the Government. These have become increasingly granular, with the latest one covering the *UK Plan for Tackling Roadside Nitrogen Dioxide Concentrations 2017*.[102] In this case Mr Justice Garnham ordered the Government to supplement the plan in respect of 45 of the 389 local authorities (note not zones) where exceedances were likely to occur for a further two years, to 'ensure that … steps are taken to achieve compliance as soon as possible, by the quickest route possible and by a means that makes that outcome likely'.[103] The specific upshot of the litigation is the recent ministerial direction under the Environment Act 1995 to councils marginally in breach of NO_2 standards to speed up studies of solutions.[104]

---

[101] *R (ClientEarth) v Secretary of State for the Environment* [2011] EWHC 3623 ('*Client Earth (No 1)*'. The full list is completed by *R (ClientEarth) v Secretary of State for the Environment* [2012] EWCA Civ 897; *R (ClientEarth) v Secretary of State for the Environment* [2013] UKSC 25 and [2015] UKSC 28; *R (ClientEarth (No 2)) v Secretary of State for the Environment* [2016] EWHC 2740 (Admin); *R (ClientEarth (No 3)) v Secretary of State for the Environment, Secretary of State for Transport, and Welsh Ministers* [2018] EWHC 315 (Admin).

[102] Her Majesty's Government, *UK Plan for Tackling Roadside Nitrogen Dioxide Concentrations: Detailed Plan* (DEFRA/DoT 2017).

[103] *Client Earth (No 3)* [74].

[104] Environment Act 1995 (Feasability Study for Nitrogen Dioxide Compliance) Air Quality Direction 2018.

Britain, then, is now tackling the issue with a degree of urgency that has been lacking, but in doing so it is putting into perspective the tardy response of the European Commission. Consider in this regard the Commission's Air Quality Impact Assessment 2013,[105] in which it impressed upon Member States the importance of compliance in terms of public health. With fuller compliance, the Commission was confident that the 406,000 deaths in the EU attributable to air pollution could be reduced to 340,000 in 2020, working towards eliminating deaths altogether. But the Commission lacked a plan, and it lacked a sense of urgency. Tragically, but unsurprisingly, in *Air Quality in Europe – 2017 Report*, 502,000 deaths are attributed to particles, nitrogen and ozone.[106]

A recent appraisal of the 2008 Directive identifies two main problems, which illustrate shortcomings in EU governance:[107] first, widespread failure of Member States to comply with the Directive; and second, 'failure of the legislation itself to achieve the ... policy objective of bringing down the value of key air pollutants below the WHO guidelines'.[108] These are of course connected. The Commission has sought to confer binding legal status on the substance of the WHO guidelines, without addressing the reasons why, in the international context, they are intended to operate morally and politically. The guidelines speak to levels of air pollutant that are safe, in a wider context of social, economic and cultural considerations that gainsay the achievement of clean air. In pursuing a strategy of 'legislating away' harmful pollutants, the Commission and wider EU actors have above all harmed confidence in rule of law, as the RCEP anticipated.

However, can it really be argued that Britain, leaving the EU, should take the opportunity to strip back the domestic effect of the WHO guidelines to their being just that – guidelines? Whilst the Royal Commission's prophecy of difficulties has been vindicated, it recommendations arguably have not. Quite apart from the fact that binding standards are now in place, and that Britain is on course to comply with them earlier

---

[105] European Commission, *Impact Assessment*, SWD (2013) 531. 27. See E Fasoli, 'Review and Adjustment under the UN ECE Transboundary Air Pollution Treaty Regimes and Implementation of EU Legislation' (2017) 26 *European Energy and Environmental Law Review* 30.

[106] European Environment Agency, *Air Quality in Europe – 2017 Report* (EEA 2017) table 10.1.

[107] S Varvastian, 'Achieving the EU Air Policy Objectives in Due Time: A Reality or a Hoax?' (2015) 24 *European Energy and Environmental Law Review* 2.

[108] ibid 11.

than, say, Germany (or France), it is unclear that the Royal Commission was right.[109] The argument against the Royal Commission is that binding standards are appropriate, so long as they command the respect of the public, and provided the governmental institutions out of which they emerge and by which they are policed acknowledge, with Edith Summerskill, the importance of the 'human touch'.[110] In that respect it is significant that the majority of local authorities complied with the 2005 deadline under the 1995 Act.

III. CONCLUSION

Local air pollution problems lend themselves in principle particularly well to EU competence. This is not because roadside pollutants have a substantial transboundary character, or that ill-health is a barrier to trade. Rather, it is because, ever since Britain joined the EU, the main sources of urban air pollution have shifted from factories and homes to emissions from cars, vans and lorries. In principle, this is a subject matter over which Member States have considerably more control acting together than acting alone. In practice, however, the scope for cleaner air has been frustrated by the structural tension within the EU Treaty order between a commitment to a high standard of environmental protection and a commitment to sustained economic growth. Fossil fuel transport has been an economic success for the EU, and is going from strength to strength. Volkswagen has brushed off the corruption scandal to overtake Toyota as the world's biggest car manufacturer on some calculations, whilst Renault (or Renault-Nissan) is not far behind. In its *Wheels within Wheels* campaign, Friends of the Earth was critical of the disproportionate influence of the car manufacturing lobby on politicians.[111] Today, that applies more to the EU than Britain.

Yet air pollution is not simply a matter of industry capture of politicians. Like the pokeable companionable fire, the fossil fuel car is a source of pollution that has captured the public imagination throughout the world. It is intertwined with aesthetics, comfort, and convenience and, broadly, culture. There is talk as Britain leaves the EU of a (new) Clean Air Act, as recommended by the joint Environment, Health and Transport

---

[109] See RCEP, 5th Report, n 61.
[110] Summerskill, above n 55.
[111] M Hamer, *Wheels Within Wheels: A Study of the Road Lobby* (Friends of the Earth 1974). The book emphasises the problem of domestic motor cars and, presciently, their emissions of oxides of nitrogen (eg at 55).

Committee on the subject.[112] The original Clean Air Act rid urban air of a culturally deep-rooted source of pollution. But the price was high. In particular, it boosted the electricity generating industry, the power stations of which inspired Friends of the Earth to come up with 'dirty man of Europe' label. Fresh clean air legislation directed at incentivising battery-operated cars risks perpetuating the displacement of pollution from place to place, or medium to medium (it will place a new burden on the electricity generating sector, and have far reaching resource implications (turning lithium into a lucrative currency)). With this in mind, one of ClientEarth's most compelling suggestions is to support more active travel – aka walking – and, encouragingly, domestic political institutions appear to be listening.[113]

---

[112] *Improving Air Quality*, 4th Report of the Environment, Food and Rural Affairs Committee, 4th Report of the Environmental Audit Committee, 3rd Report of the Health and Social Care Committee, 2nd Report of the Transport Committee, Session 2017/2018 (HC 433).
[113] DEFRA Select Committee et al, *Improving Air Quality*, Session 2017–2019, HC 433 (Stationery Office) (esp 92); and see ClientEarth Written Evidence.

6

Habitat Conservation

THE HEBRIDEAN ISLE of Islay is world-renowned for a single malt
whisky, called Laphroaig, marketed for its unique peaty flavour.
The flavour comes from ancient bogs, like Duich Moss, fertilised
by the droppings of the Greenland White Fronted Goose.[1] Islay is a
particularly appropriate starting point for the final case study, because
there can have been few visitors to the island over the ages as rare as
Commission-official/scholar Ludwig Kramer, investigating a complaint
of breach of Community environmental law. The complaint was brought
by the Royal Society for the Protection of Birds (RSPB), alleging Britain's
failure to fulfil its obligations under the Wild Birds Directive 1979.[2] Its
basis was that the local planning authority had granted planning permission for a new tranche of peat extraction from Duich Moss, which
would interfere with one of the Earth's principal winter habitats of the
Greenland Goose. Kramer was investigating whether the bog should be
designated under the Directive.

Usually, the European Commission responds to allegations of breach
of Community law by writing to the Member State asking for an explanation. In this case, however, Kramer, as Nigel Haigh puts it, 'decided to
go and see for himself':[3]

> Nothing like this had ever happened before in the EC. Did the official have
> the right to come? Was his visit desirable? Could he be stopped if he insisted
> on coming? ... There was no doubt that the official could visit Islay as a

---

[1] M Holdgate, *Penguins and Mandarins: The Memoirs of Martin Holdgate* (Memoir
Club 2003) 236.

[2] Council Directive 79/409/EEC on the conservation of wild birds [1979] OJ L103/1. For
an overview of the complaint, see N Haigh, 'The European Community and International
Environmental Policy' in A Hurrell and B Kingbury (eds), *The International Politics of the
Environment* (Oxford University Press 1992) 230–33.

[3] Haigh, n 2, 232. Kramer has written of the exceptional nature of site visits: 'visits [to]
places of presumed breach of environmental provisions are not more frequent than once
per year on average' (L Kramer, *Focus on European Environmental Law*, 2nd edn (Sweet &
Maxwell 1997) 6).

holiday maker to watch birds, but he was intending to come as a repre-
sentative of the ... institution that is the guardian of the Treaty, in order to
investigate a complaint, by a private body, against a Member State for failure
to fulfil an obligation under the Treaty.[4]

In the event, the Foreign Office welcomed Kramer, and a diplomatic
crisis was averted.

This chapter focuses on issues arising from the 'Was his visit desirable?' question. As Brexit is driven above all by the narrative of national
independence, Kramer's enforcement action might be considered from
this standpoint an illustration of the repatriation of power over habitats
from which Britain might benefit. There is no official account of the visit,
and thus no record of its outcome. What is clear is that the dispute was
settled amicably, as the company found an alternative source of peat that
was less controversial but no less fragrant. Subsequently, the Duich Moss
site was designated under the Birds Directive and simultaneously the
Ramsar Convention,[5] then under the Habitats Directive[6] and, finally, as
a National Nature Reserve under domestic legislation.[7] Tellingly, at the
time of Kramer's visit, Duich Moss was already a site of special scientific interest (SSSI), designated under a legislative scheme originating in
the National Parks and Access to the Countryside Act 1949. The site
was subject to two habitat conservation agreements, each for a term of
980 years.

The topic of habitat protection is understood by Friends of the Earth
as the most at-risk aspect of the environment as Britain leaves the EU.[8]
Exiting the Birds and Habitats Directives is assessed as 'very high risk'
on every Brexit scenario.[9] This chapter offers an alternative perspective. Whilst Kramer's dramatic intervention put pressure on Britain to
designate the site under Community law, it is by no means clear that
it was decisive in doing so, or, crucially, what practical protection the
Community designation added to the pre-existing domestic one. What
the official visit did reveal, however, is that the European Commission

---

[4] Haigh, n 2, 232.

[5] Convention on Wetlands of International Importance Especially as a Wildfowl Habitat
1971, [1971] 11 *ILM* 693 (Ramsar Convention).

[6] Council Directive 92/43/EEC on the Conservation of Natural Habitats and Wild Flora
and Fauna [1992] OJ L206/7.

[7] The regulatory site history is available at 'Site Details for Eilean na Muice Duibhe
(Duich Moss), Islay', available at http://gateway.snh.gov.uk/sitelink/siteinfo.jsp?pa_
code=8494.

[8] C Burns, V Gravey and A Jordan, *UK Environmental Policy Post-Brexit: A Risk Assessment* (Friends of the Earth 2017).

[9] ibid 7.

considers itself as having the power to enter Britain to monitor compliance with EU law, and that its exercise is a matter of considerable political delicacy. If (as is common) the Commission refrains from using this power, in an act of self-censorship, how can it be discharging its constitutional obligation of guardianship of the Treaty? If it does use this power, to whom is it accountable, in a way comparable to that which legitimates the police powers of domestic agencies?

Exiting the EU habitats conservation regime, I argue, is a positive step, for reasons that are centrally connected to the above dilemma. The Duich Moss case highlights the sense in which the European Commission is caught between the rock and a hard place of remote desk-top processing of investigations of complaints, on the one hand, and a more proactive role in which the Commission risks coming across as a 'foreign power', on the other. The Commission took Britain by surprise, and risked a diplomatic incident, the political fallout from which could have been damaging. There is also a question of the tactics of the RSPB in invoking EU law. Complaints are free, but that is also true of a request to the Scottish Secretary to revoke the planning permission using executive powers.[10] The organisation was also well enough resourced to seek to quash the permission on an application for judicial review.[11]

I. THE BRITISH WAY OF HABITAT CONSERVATION 1945–73

Habitat conservation is a topic that strongly engages the British way of environmental protection as a post-war phenomenon, for the purposes of my book's historical approach to Brexit. Subsumed within the language of 'countryside', habitats played a pivotal part in War Office and Ministry of Information propaganda. Servicemen and women were exhorted to lay their lives on the line for Britain's 'green and pleasant land' and, as a consequence, according to Marion Shoard, there was at this time 'more concentrated reflection on the future of countryside than ever occurred before'.[12] The focus here is on two major Acts aimed at general

---

[10] As happened following *R v Secretary of State for the Environment, ex parte BeeBee* [1991] 2 PLR 27.

[11] As the site was protected under the Countryside Act 1968 and the National Parks and Access to the Countryside Act 1949, there seems a reasonable chance of the planning grant's being successfully challenged by means of judicial review, and/or through political pressure to be put on the company, whether by the Government (with the threat of a power to revoke the permission) or by the landlord (under private law).

[12] M Shoard, *Right to Roam* (Oxford University Press 1999) 184.

protection of the countryside (Town and Country Planning Act 1947) and those especially cherished features of it (National Parks and Access to the Countryside Act (NPACA) 1949), that arose out of this concentrated reflection.

A. Green and Pleasant Land: Soldiers and Ecologists in Post-war Britain

The wartime propaganda referred to above revolved around an initiative called 'Your Britain: Fight for it Now'. This was the strapline for a series of paintings the Government commissioned from Frank Newbould in 1942, to boost national morale.[13] The images depict pastoral farming in rolling landscapes,[14] a village pub and green,[15] a church in pleasing grounds,[16] and a fair.[17] All are bucolic, evoking an idyllic, cooperative relationship between society and wider nature. There are, tellingly, no tall mountains or dark forests, not because Britain lacked landscapes of that sort, but because most people (so the Government calculated) were more inspired by nature as a home rather than a wilderness. This was the general context of the Labour Government's policy for 'the conservation of nature' in England and Wales and Scotland, set out in respective White Papers in 1947.[18]

There are various strands to the politics underlying the countryside to draw out, in order to capture the emergence of a British way of habitat protection. One is access, or rather public access. This has a long history, including the work done by the Commons, Open Spaces and Footpaths Preservation Society (established in 1865) to ameliorate obstacles to access arising from enclosure of the land, and, between the wars, the Workers Sports Federation, which organised the Kinder Scout mass trespass on 24 April 1932.[19] However, some of the most powerful 'campaigning' was by example, taking the form of townsfolk choosing

---

[13] P Ayers, *Shaping Ecology: The Life of Arthur Tansley* (Wiley-Blackwell 2012) 6.
[14] South Downs (No 1), Art IWM PST 0069; South Downs (No 2), Art IWM PST 14887.
[15] Village Green, Art IWM PST 3641.
[16] Salisbury Cathedral, Art IWM PST 3640.
[17] Alfriston Fair, Art IWM PST 8915.
[18] *Conservation of Nature in England and Wales*, Cm 7122 (HMSO 1947); *National Parks and the Conservation of Nature in Scotland*, Cm 7235 (HMSO 1947).
[19] A proletarian rambler who was not at these protests, but who was a big influence in the Labour Party in relation to the legislation in this field, was Aneurin Bevan. Reputed to have rehearsed important speeches in the hills above the valley where he grew up, 'Nye' Bevan boasted in Parliament of his unparalleled knowledge of the flora of the South Wales hills: 'Rural Wales', HC Deb 8 December 1953, vol 521, cols 1822–1929, col 1903.

in their growing leisure time to enjoy the countryside surrounding towns and cities. Marion Shoard (again) evokes a particularly quaint scene of 'young shop and office workers' cycling on the Peak's paths, 'sometimes being followed by their parents on tandems'.[20]

A second strand to the politics of post-war conservation concerns the perceived health-bestowing benefits of communing with nature, physically, mentally and spiritually. This is a reflection of the influential 'progressive' group that grew up around nature-loving patricians such as the 3rd Earl Russell (Bertrand Russell) and George Macaulay Trevelyan, professional scientists including Julian Huxley and Arthur Tansley, the architect John Dower and the Etonian Labour Party politician Hugh Dalton. As David Cannadine explains, this powerful set, which advocated greater government planning in all spheres, 'came to prefer the ethics of Wordsworth to Jesus Christ' and 'to believe that walking long distances in the countryside was the essential path to mystical experience, to mental ecstasy and to spiritual enlightenment'.[21] Keith Thomas, in his study of Trevelyan's legacy, singles out the work of 1931 entitled *The Call and Claims of Natural Beauty* for its eloquence,[22] but Trevelyan's *Illustrated English Social History*[23] was a more influential companion to the pastoral imagery of the artist Newbould. The challenge, on this paradigm, was to reconnect the working population with the country life from which industrialisation removed them.

A third strand concerns the ecological significance of the countryside. This was articulated above all by Tansley, the founding President of the British Ecological Society (BES).[24] He advocated government-owned or government-managed nature reserves in which what he called 'ecosystems' could be studied in 'real world' laboratories. According to Tansley, because of their complexity, ecosystems could only be understood on a system-wide scale, over time. Tansley's saw nature reserves as part of a more general planned land use regime. He argued for

[s]ome form of national planning of a systematic 'lay-out' of the whole country, in which various interests are duly considered and adjusted – the

---

[20] Shoard, n 12, 177. On a typical spring Sunday, 15,000 daytrippers from Sheffield alone would travel to the Peaks, whilst Manchester Piccadilly train station would have queues of ramblers stretching along the roads, destined for the Peak District.

[21] D Cannadine, *GM Trevelyan: A Life in History* (Harper Collins 1992) 145.

[22] GM Trevelyan, *The Call and Claims of Natural Beauty* (Hazel, Watson and Viney 1931), cited in K Thomas, *Man and the Natural World: Changing Attitudes in England 1500–1800* (Allen Lane 1983) 14.

[23] GM Trevelyan, *Illustrated English Social History, Vol 4* (Longman 1952).

[24] See Ayers, n 13; and P Anker, *Imperial Ecology: Environmental Order in the British Empire, 1895–1945* (Harvard University Press 2001) esp 8–40.

rural as well as the urban, the spiritual and the aesthetic, as well as the industrial and commercial.[25]

He became the first Director of the UK-wide research and regulatory body, Nature Conservancy, created by Royal Charter in 1949.

This, then, is an extremely complex political milieu, in which the beginnings of a body of regulatory law relating to habitats were shaped by grand narratives of industrialisation, secularisation and democratisation. John Sheail summed up the intriguing combination of progressivism and nostalgia in the strands of thought here noted as being 'to secure a landscape that was both historic and modern'.[26] A good place to start with the exposition of the law is with property, and the intriguing way in which the old 'country estate' was reinvented as an answer to the habitat conservation needs of modernity.

B. The Common Law Property Context of Statutory Intervention

The post-war statutory framework for the conservation of nature was laid upon significant common law provisions relating to property in land. Gerd Winter is one of the many who have written about the 'Janus character' of property rights as they concern habitats – as both a potential obstacle to regulatory law (the right to property is sometimes used to challenge the legality of regulation) and, at the same time, as a powerful private means of conservation with which the wider public interest is bound up.[27] His most significant contribution is to highlight the German juridical concept of *Situationsgebundenheit*, which denotes a 'situation bond', in which the proprietor is bound by the physical and historical constraints of the site. These constraints are temporal (the legacy of previous owners) and spatial (the interests of neighbours). Winter refers to a 1950s case in which 'every landed

---

[25] A Tansley, *The British Islands and their Vegetation* (Cambridge University Press 1939) 192. Another explanation for Tansley's influence within the intelligentsia is his polymathic literacy in the discipline of psychology. He was one of the first to engage with the work of Freud, and switched readily between the ecology and psychology disciplines. He understood the discipline of ecology through a psychological lens, as a quest of the individual to reconcile the mind with the complexity of world's matter and physical forces (see Anker, n 24, 29–31).

[26] J Sheail, *An Environmental History of Twentieth-Century Britain* (Palgrave 2002) 115.

[27] G Winter, 'Property Rights and Nature Conservation' in C-H Born, A Cliquet, H Schoukens, D Misonne and G Van Hoorick (eds), *The Habitat Directive in its EU Environmental Law Context: European Nature's Best Hope?* (Routledge 2015) 215, 224–25.

property is characterized by its location ... [and] embeddedness in landscape and nature'.[28]

This resonates with property law in Britain. As suggested in chapter 2, the jurisdictions of England and Wales and Scotland have a broadly similar concept that is inherent in the law and practice of estates in land.[29] The BES report authored by Tansley advocated Nation Nature Reserves as a surrogate for the private nature reserves ordered through trust and trust-like ownership of land, which Tansley could not see as having any future politically:[30]

> In the age of large private estates, which frequently included beautiful scenery, destructive development was often effectively prevented by the pride of owners in their possessions and their frequent refusal to part with or lease their land even when this would have been extremely profitable ... Now that we are passing into a time when the wealth and power of large landowners will probably be increasingly and drastically curtailed, this precarious safeguard of rural beauty will disappear and public action becomes the only means by which it can be preserved.[31]

However, Tansley exaggerated the vulnerability of the British landed establishment.[32]

The relationship between the Labour Party and the landed elite is both fascinating and important. Tansley was thinking of the anti-establishment attitudes of the Edwardian Liberal administrations of Herbert Asquith and David Lloyd George. However, in the changing political climate, the Labour Party adopted a pragmatic line. It saw some value in patrician patterns of landownership. In the chapter of *The Environmental Revolution* covering 'The British Story', Max Nicholson set out the 'great merits' of the landed estate, in which 'land itself was

---

[28] Citing BGHZ 60, 124 (134); LM art 14 GG Nr 60, DOV 1957, 669 (ibid 224).

[29] For a different treatment, emphasising the exploitative aspects of the common law of property rights, see C Rodgers, *The Law of Nature Conservation: Property, Environment and the Limits of Law* (Oxford University Press 2013) 25–32.

[30] British Ecological Society, 'Report of the Committee: Nature Conservation and Nature Reserves' (1944) 32 *Journal of Ecology* 45.

[31] ibid 47. See more generally AN Wilson, *After the Victorians 1901–1953* (Hutchinson 2010) 319 (commenting on the openness of the British landed aristocracy to Labour Party politicians, illustrated by elevation of weaver's son Philip Snowden to a hereditary peerage (Viscount Snowden)). 'In spite of state socialism of Attlee's government, the House of Lords went on, the huge bulk of land continued to be owned by the old landed class' – a phenomenon Wilson describes as 'bizarre' (ibid 518). See further n 37 and associated text.

[32] The Labour Party, in *Let Us Face the Future* (1945), committed to 'land nationalization', but what did that mean? The Town and Country Planning Act 1947 nationalised the right to develop land, but the land itself remained held by individuals of the Crown.

handled with a sense of the interdependent relationship between man and nature'.[33] Nicholson claims that estates handed down over generations represent a laudably 'organic approach' to landownership, which is the 'antithesis of the distorted and artificial approach of classical economics'.[34] In the Socialist Commonwealth of Great Britain, hereditary proprietors are benevolent protectors of natural and cultural heritage rather than 'takers' as portrayed, above all, by Lloyd George.

It is possible to identify key figures in this transformation, notably GM Trevelyan. A 'new Liberal' before the Great War, he supported Lloyd George's Land Campaign and the Parliament Act 1911, which ended the co-equality of the hereditary and elected chambers of Parliament. However, he came to regret the Campaign and its contribution to the break-up of patrician estates.[35] He believed that 'standards of public life had declined, the beauty of the countryside had been eroded and the worth of "spiritual values" had been questioned'.[36] After 1945, Trevelyan sought to make amends. He worked with Lord Zetland, Lord Crawford and Lord Wemyss to help expand the National Trust. He saw this as a leftist venture, consistent with 'admiration for Hugh Dalton's [Fabian] environmental endeavours'.[37] Hugh Dalton, likewise, admired Trevelyan's work with the National Trust, which he regarded as a 'typically British example of practical socialism in action'.[38]

When Britain entered the Community this leftist defence of the country estate converged with more politically conservative thinking to exert considerable influence. National Trust membership went from 158,000 in 1965 to 539,000 in 1975, and to a million by 1981 (a rate of growth that saw it top 5 million members more recently). Mark Girouard captures the public mood in his books about the physical and social aspects of stately homes, including the gothic mind-set of their custodians.[39] As Dominic Sandbrook explains, Britain entered the Community in the thrall of the 'cult of the past';[40] both 'high and low culture seemed

---

[33] M Nicholson, *The Environmental Revolution: A Guide for the New Masters of the Earth* (Hodder and Stoughton 1970) 149.

[34] ibid. See further ch 2.

[35] Cannadine, n 21, 178

[36] ibid.

[37] ibid 178–79.

[38] B Pimlott, *Hugh Dalton: A Life* (Jonathan Cape 1985) 456.

[39] M Girouard, *Hardwick Hall: A Brief Guide* (National Trust 1977); M Girouard, *Life in the English Country House* (Yale University Press 1978); M Girouard, *Return to Camelot: Chivalry and the English Gentleman* (Yale University Press 1981); M Girouard, *A Country House Companion* (Yale University Press 1987).

[40] D Sandbrook, *State of Emergency: Britain 1970–1974* (Allen and Lane 2010) 196.

saturated with nostalgia'.[41] Roy Strong wrote of 'Britain's environmental heritage ... represent[ing] some form of security, a point of reference, a refuge perhaps, something visible and tangible which, within a topsy turvy world, seems stable and unchanged'.[42]

C. Regulatory Law: Acts of 1947 and 1949

Regulatory law in the field of habitat protection evolved, in accordance with Tansley's thinking,[43] within the general framework of land use control under the 1947 Act, rather than as substantially freestanding provisions of the kind that operated in areas of pollution control.[44] Part of the reason for this is the accident of history by which the planning regime post-dated statutory pollution control, whilst pre-dating statutory habitat conservation law.[45] But it is also because almost all habitats in Britain are fundamentally part of the 'built' environment, being shaped by anthropogenic land uses.[46] A well-functioning town and control planning regime, it was thought, would give appropriate weight to habitat protection in the context of all other material considerations relating to the development of land, with some help from habitat-specialist agencies, working under the 1949 Act.

The meaning of 'well-functioning' in this context has many layers, which it is important to identify in order to appreciate why habitat protection was entrusted to the town and country planning regime, and has largely remained so. One concerns the professionalisation of town and country planning officers, through the work of Royal Town Planning Institute (RTPI) in educating planning professionals, formulating and enforcing professional standards of conduct, and facilitating critical

[41] ibid 197.

[42] ibid 196–97 (referring to the citation of Strong in P Cormack, *Heritage in Danger* (Quartet Books 1978) 10).

[43] Tansley, n 25.

[44] See C Rodgers, 'Planning and Nature Conservation: Law in the Service of Biodiversity' in C Miller (ed), *Planning an Environmental Protection* (Hart Publishing 2001) 91, where it is noted that the 1949 Act was 'primarily based in planning law', and that the 'emergence of a discrete body of "nature conservation law" is a development of more recent provenance'.

[45] See M Grant, *Urban Planning Law* (Sweet & Maxwell 1982) 5ff; and more generally W Ashworth, *The Genesis of Modern Town Planning* (Routledge 1954).

[46] John Dower, echoing Trevelyan, Tansley, and friends, wrote in his report for the Government of a British habitat as 'the joint product of nature and human use over many generations; it cannot be preserved in anything like its present aspect unless the human use is kept going' (J Dower, *National Parks in England and Wales*, Cm 6378 (HMSO 1945)).

reflection on practice.[47] Another is the role played by elected local councillors and the wider political constituencies that participate (or not) in the planning process. Then there are the further complexities of the relationship between local and central government, involving political supervision of local planning exercised by the Planning Minister and the conventions of responsible government within which they operate.

From a legal perspective, the 'well-functioning' planning regime is framed by administrative laws of various kinds (notably statutory appeals against the refusal of permission, judicial review of the grant of permission) and property law. Planning permission removes an administrative obstacle to the exploitation of land but not any proprietary ones.[48] The developer must have a private right to develop, and in exercising that right must respect the reciprocal entitlement of a neighbour protected by nuisance law. But that is not to suggest a clear divide between political and legal frameworks. As Patrick McAuslan argued, administrative law processes are informed by competing 'ideologies',[49] relating to property, public interest and public participation. This can just as easily apply to private law. Across the spectrum of public and private law are, at any one time, protagonists addressing claims relating to private property in land, regulatory discretion and 'unofficial' public opinion.[50]

The NPACA 1949 was intended to sit within this sophisticated, legal-political overarching regulatory regime, by providing a steer as to the habitats of particular public interest and to which planning authorities should attribute appropriate weight. The signature designation, albeit that it applied only to England and Wales, was 'national park', which implemented the reports of John Dower[51] and Arthur Hobhouse.[52] It is

---

[47] With an original membership of 115, by 1960 the RTPI had over 4,000 members. The RTPI devised the first professional town-planning syllabus in 1916, and edited the *Town Planning Review*. See G Cherry, *The Evolution of British Town Planning: A History of Town Planning in the United Kingdom During the 20th Century of the Royal Institute of Town Planning, 1914–1974* (Leonard Hill Books 1974). Another dimension to this is the professionalisation of Nature Conservancy, which started out life as a group of eminent ecologists pursuing, in the course of public service, personal causes and research interests, with the boundary between public and private here, as elsewhere, being profoundly blurred. See further Holdgate, at n 87 and associated text; and Ayers, n 11, 155–70.

[48] For a significant judgment covering the interface between planning and private property, see *Coventry v Lawrence* [2014] UKSC 13.

[49] P McAuslan, *The Ideologies of Planning Law* (Pergamon Press 1980).

[50] On the role of ideology (or culture) within the law more generally, see the socio-legal perspective of Karl Llewellyn, in ch 1, n 5 and associated text.

[51] Dower, n 46.

[52] A Hobhouse, *Report of the National Park Committee (England and Wales)*, Cm 6628 (HMSO 1947).

interesting to note, in relation to the previous section, that the equivalent report for Scotland envisaged public ownership of national parks, but that underestimated the power of the landed interest, both economically and also rhetorically: Scottish landlords, like their English and Welsh counterparts, saw themselves as ancestral custodians of the land, and argued (as above) that they were effective guardians of nature.[53] Other designations to note are 'national nature reserves' (NNRs),[54] 'sites of special scientific interest' (SSSIs),[55] 'open country'[56] and 'areas of outstanding natural beauty' (AONBs).[57]

Of these designations, the national park is the most ambitious in terms of seeking to integrate the values or interests of access, physical, mental, spiritual and aesthetic development of the individual, and ecological knowledge and well-being. Designations are the responsibility of the Secretary of State, acting on the recommendations of the competent national advisory authority (then the National Parks Commission). Unusually for a domestic statute, the purposes for which a designation is to be made are set out in the primary legislation, viz 'conserving and enhancing the natural beauty, wildlife and cultural heritage of the areas', and 'promoting opportunities for the understanding and enjoyment of the special qualities of those areas by the public.'[58] The importance of public access is highlighted by the requirement that in proposing a designation, the competent authority must take into account proximity to urban populations for purposes of accessibility.[59] This made the Peak District an appropriate inaugural designation, confirmed by Hugh Dalton (Secretary of State), on 17 April 1951.[60]

---

[53] The Ramsay Committee had recommended that these sites be acquired by the Government for the nation, which Scots landowners rejected (and the parks idea was recast as an administrative provision). See Scottish National Parks Survey Committee, *National Parks: A Scottish Survey*, Cm 6631 (HMSO 1945).

[54] NPACA 1949, pt III.

[55] ibid s 23.

[56] ibid s 59.

[57] ibid s 87.

[58] ibid s 5.

[59] On the need for the land to be accessible, see *Meyrick Estate Management Ltd v Secretary of State for the Environment, Food and Rural Affairs* [2007] EWCA Civ 523.

[60] It was selected because of its being no more than an hour by rail from a population of 16m. The full list of designations and their dates is Peak District (17 April 1951), Lake District (9 May 1951), Snowdonia (18 October 1951), Dartmoor (30 October 1951), Pembrokeshire (29 February 1952), North Yorkshire Moors (29 November 1952), Exmoor (19 October 1954), Yorkshire Dales (16 November 1954), Northumberland (6 April 1956), Brecon Beacons (17 April 1957), Norfolk Broads (1 April 1989), New Forest (1 March 2005), South Downs (31 March 2010). Equivalent sites in Scotland were called

The most singularly ecological designations are NNRs and SSSIs. The former are designated and managed by the competent authority (then Nature Conservancy) for purposes of research into and/or preservation of 'the fauna and flora of Great Britain and the physical conditions in which they live'.[61] Intriguingly, SSSIs were at this initial stage presented as a step down from NNRs,[62] in that they were merely notifications to the planning authority that a site was of ecological significance. The owners would be informed by Nature Conservancy as a matter of good practice, but the statute did not require them to be, nor did it empower conservation agreements between the Conservancy and the site's proprietor. Thus Jack Garner, in his leading text on the Act, did not consider SSSIs worthy of a mention.[63] However, within three years of the Act, 1,314 notifications of SSSIs were made,[64] as the Conservancy exploited the simplicity and the economy of this tool. In time the Conservancy was empowered under a later Act to enter into SSSI management agreements,[65] but by this time they were already capable of being described as the 'key legal protection for nature conservation'[66] or, as the Joint Nature Conservation Committee quaintly refers to them, the 'jewels in the UK's nature conservation crown'.[67]

Two further designations are worth briefly noting, to reinforce the sense of an attempt on the part of Parliament to recognise the nuances of habitat protection and its many different settings, and the underlying political interests and goals. One is 'open country', which is designated by local planning authorities to provide people with access to the countryside on the outskirts of conurbations. As the law and practice

'high amenity areas', or 'National Park Direction Areas', designated under the 1947 Act by the Scottish Secretary. These corresponded to the sites recommended by the Report by the Ramsay Committee, ie Loch Lommond-Trossachs; Glen Affric-Glen Cannich-Strath Farrar; Ben Nevis-Glen Coe-Black Mount; the Cairngorms; Loch Torridon-Loch Maree-Loch Broom. Under the National Parks (Scotland) Act 2000, there are two designations: Loch Lommond and Trossach (2002); the Cairngorms (2003).

[61] NPACA 1949, s 15.

[62] ibid s 23.

[63] It is the only one of the five designations not to receive a mention in the discussion of the 1949 Act in J Garner, *The Public Control of Land* (Sweet & Maxwell 1959) 39ff. Subsequently, a further noteworthy designation, 'Country Park', was introduced under the Countryside (Scotland) Act 1967 and the Countryside Act 1968.

[64] HC Deb 28 June 1954, vol 529, col 77W (figures as of 19 June 1954).

[65] Countryside Act 1968, s 15.

[66] S Ball, 'Reforming the Law of Habitats Protection' in C Rodgers (ed), *Nature Conservation and Countryside Law* (University of Wales Press 1996) 89.

[67] Joint Nature Conservation Committee, 'Monitoring Protected Sites', available at http://jncc.defra.gov.uk/page-3847-theme=print.

unfolded, this proved the least useful, or least used, of the 1949 Act designations.[68] The other is the AONB designation, which is an aesthetically focused designation that does not require public access (in contrast to national parks and open country).[69] Also of note is the designation, this time under the 1947 Act, of green-belt land. This 'took off' with Duncan Sandys' Green Belt Circular of 1955.[70] Over time the green belt has grown to cover about one-fifth of Britain's territory.[71]

To reiterate, all these designations ultimately share the important design feature of their subordination to town and country planning regulation. Sheail rightly captures the 1949 Act as a mainly declaratory measure.[72] That is to say, the normative force of the protection derives from the political-moral authority of the judgement (by the Minister, or Nature Conservancy and so on) that the site has a particular value to weigh against others. There is no absolute, or near absolute, formal protection, partly because the emphasis is on the force of the designation per se, and also because, in more formal legal terms, a planning authority cannot fetter its discretion by adopting a blanket policy against (or for) development. Furthermore, and problematically, many of the threats to the ecology of designated habitats lie outside of the planning regime,[73] notably changes in agricultural use, including afforestation or deforestation, or simply allowing the site to fall into disuse. In these circumstances, the value of the designation is *purely* 'politically-moral', resting on the proprietor's willingness to respect the designation (with the help of pressure arising from, as it were, the de facto 'situation bond').[74]

A related aspect to emphasise is the pivotal role of voluntary action. This is what the sponsoring Minister (John Silkin) had to say about the Bill he knew had cross-party support:

> This Bill is the culmination of the pioneering efforts of many public spirited persons who devoted themselves to the open-air cause through the agency of voluntary organisations. Some of them were formed as far back as the second half of the last century. If I may, I should like to mention some of the names of these organisations, and in doing so I hope I am not leaving out any

---

[68] Part of the obstacle is that the definition is narrow, referring specifically to mountain, moor, heath, down, cliff or foreshore (including any bank, barrier, dune, beach, flat or other land adjacent to the foreshore): see s 59(2).

[69] See further Garner, n 63, 33.

[70] Ministry of Housing and Local Government Circular 42/55.

[71] B Clapp, *Environmental History of Britain* (Longman 1994) 140.

[72] Above n 26.

[73] Rodgers, n 44, 92

[74] Above n 25.

body which ought to be mentioned. There is the Council for the Preservation of Rural England, the Commons, Open Spaces and Footpaths Preservation Society, the Ramblers' Association, the Cyclists' Touring Club, the Youth Hostels Association and many others.[75]

The Royal Society for the Protection of Birds (established in 1889) is perhaps the biggest omission from this list, and another is the Society for the Promotion of Nature Reserves (established in 1912, and now the Royal Society of Wildlife Trusts).

Of all the measures of the post-war Labour Administration regarding the environment, habitat conservation perhaps contributes most to the revisionist strand in the literature that emphasises the ambivalence of the Labour Party towards the notion of the 'welfare state'.[76] The welfare state was a pejorative term, in so far as it denoted state control over the social sphere at the expense of people's taking responsibility for their actions. The adherence across the British 'left' and 'right' to individual responsibility for environmental protection is what gave policy and law in the field of the environment its cross-partisan character. The basic political differences lay in the role, within the understanding of the voluntary sector, of the economic market. In a planning context, the Labour Party pursued a policy of betterment, whereby the uplift in value of property as a result of planning permission was shared throughout the community. The Conservative Party policy promoted the economically liberal idea of the developer benefiting from profit-seeking development of land.

D. The Practical Achievements of Habitat Conservation as Britain Entered the Community

Looked at in terms of official designations, habitat conservation would appear to have benefitted considerably from the developments in policy and law discussed in the preceding sections. In 1973, 150 national nature reserves were under Nature Conservancy's management.[77] This is

---

[75] HC Deb 31 March 1949, col 1462. The primacy of the voluntary principle in habitat conservation was restated in the Sandford Report, but with the addition of a sub-principle (the Sandford Principle) that habitat conservation prevails over recreation where the two are in conflict (Department of Education and Science, *Report of the National Park Policy Review Committee* (HMSO 1974)).

[76] D Wincott, 'Images of Welfare in Law and Society: The British Welfare State in Comparative Perspective' (2011) 38 *Journal of Law and Society* 343.

[77] Graham Page (Minister for Housing and Local Government) HC Deb 3 July 1973, col 462.

in addition to the 350 nature reserves owned by voluntary organisations like the Royal Society for the Protection of Birds.[78] These covered only about 1 per cent of Britain, eclipsed by SSSIs subject to section 15 management agreements, numbering 'about 3000' (and covering roughly 6 per cent of Britain).[79] There were also 19 AONBs, covering almost 10 per cent of Britain. The three national parks of Wales covered 20 per cent of that country, with the seven English national parks covering 8 per cent of England.[80] Add to these figures the 'high amenity areas' in Scotland, and the overall picture is of an extensive body of habitat conservation as Britain entered the Community. This is strongly reinforced by the wider body of regulatory law within the framework of town and country planning, and by wider-still officially unrecorded voluntary initiatives.

But what did this mean in practice for habitats on the ground? Nature Conservancy conducted 'state of nature' surveys in 1955 and in 1965. The findings of the 1955 survey were broadly sanguine. The rationing of building materials until the early 1950s and the law of betterment (taxing profits on land development under planning permission) had indirectly protected habitats by minimising urban sprawl and development per se. Industrial agriculture had only begun to make a significant impression.[81] However, the tone of the 1965 review, eventually published for the first time – in updated form – in 1977, is more wary. It recalled two decades of human pressure, which had caused a 'rate and scale of attrition of wildlife and habitat even greater than that foreseen [by the architects of the 1947 and 1949 Acts]'.[82] Thus, whilst the present period was significant for the emergence and consolidation of post-war conservation efforts, it also corresponded to an increase in anthropogenic pressure on habitats.

[78] Page, ibid col 494.

[79] John Farr, ibid col 474.

[80] In all but Northumberland and Dartmoor, the proposed designations were confirmed in the face of deep opposition from the local authorities that would have jurisdiction over them: A and M MacEwen, *National Parks: Conservation or Cosmetics?* (Allen & Unwin 1982) 21–22.

[81] As mentioned in ch 5, the biggest immediate growth area in housing was in temporary dwellings; in terms of public infrastructure (eg hospitals), the building programme did not really 'take off' until the 1960s – the NHS operated in Victorian and Edwardian buildings. Arterial roads and housing estates were also a thing of the 1960s and beyond. In ch 2, attention has been given to the pesticide incidents, which were quite localised in the 1940s and 1950s.

[82] D Radcliffe, *The Nature Conservation Review*, vol 1: *The Selection of Biological Sites of National Importance to Nature Conservation in Great Britain* (Cambridge University Press 1977) 1.

Thus, it is understandable that general impressions of the practical impact of nature conservation over the period are rather mixed. For example, Marion Shoard, in the sentence partly quoted at the start of section I ('[wartime entailed] more concentrated reflection on the future of countryside than ever occurred before'), ends with a plaintive 'or ever again'.[83] Ann and Malcolm MacEwen (with particular reference to national parks) describe the post-war period as 'downhill (nearly) all the way',[84] referring to conservation's playing second fiddle to recreation. However, the moral authority of the national park designation explains why Friends of the Earth persuaded Rio Tinto Zinc to desist from copper mining in Snowdonia National Park in a campaign beginning in 1971.[85] Another more positive impression was given by Peter Walker at the Stockholm Conference, in positioning Britain as world leader in the field. Whilst acknowledging that the health of some habitats had been reduced by development, other healthy habitats were being gained. With the balance of nature ever changing, the most important thing for the Government was (and is) to ensure adequate monitoring of nature. Owing to Nature Conservancy's surveys of 'national capital of habitat and wildlife', arguably no country had as full an 'inventory' of the most valued sites.[86]

When it comes to assessing the practical impact of the post-war policy and law, therefore, the devil is in the detail. This is highlighted by one high-profile 'case' from late in the period, which illustrates particularly well the scope and limits of nature conservation the British way. This is a reference to the Cow Green Reservoir Case or, as Martin Holdgate refers to it, 'The Battle of Cow Green'.[87] The reservoir – it was built despite objections – is two miles long and in places a mile wide. It was constructed by the Tees Valley and Cleveland Water Board between 1967 and 1971, under the authority of a Private Act of Parliament. Its intended purpose was to supply the ICI chemical plant at Billingham

---

[83] Shoard, n 12.

[84] McEwen, n 80, 21. However, they were optimistic that the 'basic essentials for satisfactory administration' were put in place with the reorganisation of local government, to create national park authorities with development control and strategic planning powers.

[85] J Bugler, 'Friends of the Earth is 10 Years Old' *New Scientist* (30 April 1981) 294, 295; R Lamb, *Promising the Earth* (Routledge 1996) 52–53. The campaign demonstrated that mining was in principle permissible in national parks but unpopular with the public and politicians, given the authority of the national park designation – and that is why the company was persuaded to desist from its explorations.

[86] On these criteria and their subjectivity, see Radcliffe, n 82, 1–2, 172.

[87] Holdgate, n 1, 159–65.

with a reliable source of water. The original proposed site selected by the engineers of the Board was in the middle of the Moor House National Nature Reserve, designated and acquired by Nature Conservancy in 1952. The designated habitat was valued for its peaty soil, sugary limestone and alpine flora – some 'typical', some extremely 'rare'.

As Holdgate explains, the selection of the original site generated public outcry. It was also 'opposed' by Nature Conservancy. The Board's engineers responded by selecting the present site, more on the fringe of the nature reserve. Max Nicholson, the Director General of the Conservancy, was amenable to the development. He wrote an encouraging letter, saying that the reservoir might enhance the Conservancy's conservation objectives (it would provide a habitat for birds, which were his specialism). Also, it could provide a site for public recreation, thus adding to the public interest of the locality. That was the beginning of a dispute *within* the Conservancy, because Nicholson then came under pressure from organisation's rare plant specialists, two of whom resigned on the grounds that the most important feature of the site would be ruined.[88]

Holdgate, who represented the Conservancy throughout the Parliamentary proceedings into the reservoir Bill, reflects on the serious regulatory questions raised by the development and its regulatory handling:

> First, how authoritative can one be about the scientific importance of particular sites? Second, how on earth does one balance the value of a unique patch of vegetation against the need for water supplies? ... Cow Green also raised questions about how decisions are taken.[89]

The 'how decisions are taken' issue is most salient in the present context, but the first of these questions – about the lack of scientific certainty – is what lifts the 'how?' of environmental decision making above the purely technical realm. Some of the scientific criteria are technically fairly straightforward, notably 'rarity' (one criterion). Others are technically vague, notably 'typicalness', 'naturalness' and 'fragility'. Others still are not technical at all, notably 'intrinsic value'.

But as is often the case, what looked on its face to be a polarised dispute was really a matter of emphasis. It was less about reservoir versus

---

[88] The reservoir submerged half of the sugar limestone and the rare flora it supported, to strong objection not only from within the Conservancy but also among the voluntary societies with an interest in the area (ibid 161).

[89] ibid 162–63.

no reservoir (or the corollary of conservation versus no conservation) and more about the terms and conditions on which the development was going to proceed. In this instance the reservoir was approved on the condition that, at ICI's expense, the rarest plants were uprooted and relocated nearby, in the hope that there would be no 'overall' loss of conservation value. At a difficult time for Britain's industry generally, that was no small concession. Hindsight demonstrates that this was a highly constructive compromise. First, the reservoir evolved into an attractive landmark that contributed to the site's case for designation as an AONB (in 1988). Second, from an ecological perspective, it is telling that the reserve has subsequently doubled in size (it is now 7,500 hectares), and the reservoir has added to its value to birds (it is designated under the Birds Directive as a consequence). Third, the reserve is in a 'favourable' condition, as assessed by Natural England.[90]

II. THE BRITISH WAY DURING EU MEMBERSHIP

The concern in this section is with the argument that Britain's habitats have benefited from the Wild Birds and Habitats Directives, to the extent that Brexit is a 'very high risk' in every scenario.[91] The reasoning in the Friends of the Earth-commissioned assessment relies heavily on a study by scientists of the populations of birds protected by Annex 1 to the Wild Birds Directive.[92] The chief finding of the Sanderson et al study is that Annex 1 bird populations (in relation to the Wild Birds Directive) are in a healthier state compared to non-Annex 1 bird populations. However, the assessment has little to say about the quality of the EU protection of wider fauna and flora such as to justify the strong claim about the risks in this area. Furthermore, even in narrow terms of birds, the study makes no mention of the fact that wild birds are protected in

---

[90] Natural England, which owns the site, describes the reserve as famous for the rare spring gentian as well as England's largest juniper wood: 'The rare black grouse also breeds here, as does the golden plover and ring ouzel. Rare arctic-alpine plants, remnants of the ice-age, can be found and there are many species of wading birds such as lapwing, curlew, redshank and golden plover.' Natural England, Moor House – Upper Teesdale, available at https://www.gov.uk/government/publications/durhams-national-nature-reserves/durhams-national-nature-reserves#moor-house---upper-teesdale.

[91] Burns et al, n 8.

[92] F Sanderson et al, 'Assessing the Performance of EU Nature Legislation in Protecting Target Bird Species in an Era of Climate Change' (2016) 9 *Conservation Letters* 172.

parallel under EU *and* international law,[93] and through national legislation independently.

Stronger support for the argument that Brexit puts at serious risk
wildlife and habitats lies in the domestic legal scholarship of the 1990s,
published around the time of the Habitats Directive. At this time a new
generation of environmental law scholars emerged, taking a critical
view of the adequacy of established law and practice. Lynda Warren,
for example, thought that habitat conservation was a Cinderella field
compared to the higher-profile areas of pollution control that drew upon
the 'sticks' of criminal law (in contrast, habitat conservation relied on
the 'carrots' of voluntary agreements).[94] Simon Ball criticised the volun-
tariness of the regime for being ideologically driven measures 'adopted
by the Conservative Government',[95] with a 'neo-liberal' character lying
in the emphasis placed on conservation by agreement.[96] He hoped that
the Habitats Directive would entail more 'absolute' protection of designated sites.

Warren's criticism of the voluntary principle is more historically
nuanced, acknowledging that the principle goes back to the original
Labour Party architecture.[97] Her analysis is worth quoting, because it
is alive to the possibility that the British way *can* work, on these terms:

> If there is to be any significant progress using a voluntary approach to conser-
> vation it has to be through overwhelming public support. In the past this has
> been lacking. [But] voluntary environmental organisations have all seen a
> steady steep increase in membership.[98]

Garner considered that the volunteer spirit created a 'resilient' local and
national political context that pressured local planning authorities into
exercising 'restraint' in the face of applications for lucrative developments
of land,[99] whilst Peter Walker was advised that the voluntary sector did

---

[93] Notably the Berne Convention on the Conservation of European Wildlife and Natural
Habitats 1979.
[94] L Warren, 'Conservation – A Secondary Consideration' in R Churchill, L Warren and
J Gibson (eds), *Law, Policy and the Environment* (Basil Blackwell 1991). To put this in a
broader perspective, an extensive body of statutory criminal law had developed around the
protection of wild species, beginning with the Sea Birds Preservation Act 1869.
[95] Ball, n 66, 93.
[96] ibid.
[97] ibid 64.
[98] Warren, n 94, 76.
[99] See J Garner and B Jones, *Countryside Law*, 3rd end (Shaw and Sons 1997) 162:
'[T]he system, based entirely on providing "food" for informed decision making by planning authorities and relying on their exercise of planning restraint was certainly of some
value.'

most of the 'physical work actually carried out' in the field of habitat conservation.[100] The 'voluntary principle' proved particularly valuable in resolving disputes, during the 1980s, between farmers and regulators.[101]

In more recent literature the Birds/Habitats Directives have been seen as contributing a valuable level of 'new governance', sitting between local and national and international provision,[102] which Brexit threatens. In chapter 2, it was noted that the justification offered for Community competence was that Community law would be 'tougher' than domestic or international law.[103] But it seems strange to have a domestic regime built around voluntary effort and goodwill, working within a more coercive and prescriptive EU regime. One of Ludwig Kramer's most powerful points about the challenges of making Community law 'work' generally, which has particular relevance to habitats, is that the Community (this applies to the EU) has no centralised, opinion-shaping media facility, through which public opinion can be inspired around Europe's habitats.[104] It is *Member States* that have cultures linked to habitat, which differ from one another. The classic example is the juxtaposition between Germany's lore of the forest and England's trope of gentle, undulating fields.

This is why Kramer's appraisal of the prospects for EU law in this field expresses deep pessimism. In *EEC Treaty and Environmental Protection* he commented ominously (in regard to the Wild Birds Directive) that '[f]ull application of the Directive is encountering considerable difficulties in all Member States'.[105] Of attempts under the Habitats Directive to secure, by 2000, a comprehensive and effective network of protected

---

[100] Verney et al, *Fifty Million Volunteers* (HMSO 1972) 4 ('The British Trust for Conservation Volunteers now recruits well over a thousand new members per annum. These volunteers contributed in 1971 to the management of 149 sites in England, Scotland and Wales and totalled 10,270 man-days in the field').

[101] See in particular the literature on disputes over designations of SSSIs in the Somerset Levels region, which were aimed at protecting against harmful drainage schemes farmers were planning to benefit from the Common Agricultural Policy cereal subsidy. Tom King, the Environment Secretary and local Tory MP, was able to persuade farmers that SSSIs would be backed by management agreements in which the Government would fully compensate the farmers for the loss of exploitation value. See Clapp, n 71, 139; and Holdgate, n 1, 236–37.

[102] See generally C Hilson, 'The Impact of Brexit on the Environment: Exploring the Dynamics of a Complex Relationship' (2018) 7 *Journal of Transnational Environmental Law* 89, 109–12.

[103] See ch 2, n 84 and associated text.

[104] Kramer, n 3, 8.

[105] L Kramer, *EEC Treaty and Environmental Protection* (Sweet & Maxwell 1990) 14.

habitats (Natura 2000), he noted the fact of their proceeding 'extremely slowly'.[106] He likened designations of special areas of conservation (SACs) to a *peau de chagrin*; that is, with every new EU-inspired designation and its accompanying wish for better protection, the protection actually diminishes. 'Out of the battle between economical development and ecological preservation, nature in Western Europe is slowly but progressively retreating',[107] he lamented.

His recent chapter in the collection 'European Nature's Last Hope' reminds readers of Kramer's long-held view of EU habitats conservation as rather hopeless: 'the results so far confirm that assessment'.[108] Is Kramer right to be so bleak? In the passage quoted above, Kramer writes of habitat 'preservation' (the word Kramer contrasts with 'economical development'). But preservation has negative connotations in Britain, where it evokes a sense of narrow biological specialism and social and economic unemployment, as suggested by Peak District MP Arthur Molson's comments about lime mining in the National Park being necessary to fund working-class leisure time for enjoying the heritage.[109] As noted earlier, the controversial habitat battles in Britain are never really a zero sum choice between whisky or birds, or water or alpine plants; they are about having it (almost) all, somewhere, somehow. In Britain, habitats are usually said to be 'conserved', alongside the anthropogenic land uses that are among the forces shaping them.

'Member States originally considered that nature protection was their exclusive competence', Kramer wrote in *Focus on European Environmental Law*, and thus accepted Community measures 'only very reluctantly'.[110] It is easy to understand why. The Commission and the wider legislative actors (Council, Parliament) have done their utmost to nurture a sense of identity for 'EU habitats', by promoting and enforcing laws that protect habitats that reflect (the term is optimistic) 'EU heritage' and the rights of EU citizens.[111] This is evident in the *European*

---

[106] Kramer, n 3, 335.

[107] ibid 248.

[108] L Kramer, 'Implementation and Enforcement of the Habitats Directive' in Born (et al) (eds), n 27, 229, 243.

[109] 'If they [workers] require lime to earn their living on weekdays, they cannot have the whole area preserved from quarrying in order to enjoy the amenities at the week-end.' (Arthur Molson, HC Deb, above n cols 1651–52).

[110] Kramer, n 3, 334.

[111] For an early discussion of the citizenship aspect of this under the Maastricht Treaty, see R Macrory, 'Environmental Citizenship and the Law: Repairing the European Road' (1996) 8 *Journal of Environmental Law* 219.

Hamster case,[112] which centred on the near extinction of hamsters in north-east France, as a result of land-use policies that neglected to protect their habitat. These hamsters are thriving elsewhere in the EU, notably in Romania and, according to Marc Clement, in his interpretation of the ruling, the purpose of the Habitats Directive is to give Romanians, as EU citizens, a stake in the environment across the totality of Member States: 'If hamsters are no longer present in France, then this affects the right to the environment of Romanian citizens ... even if this species is abundant in Romania.'[113] He emphasises the point that 'Member States act in this domain not for themselves but for the European Union'.[114]

But the proceedings against France were controversial, because of the ambivalence of the French Government towards the EU nature conservation competence.[115] The Commission thus risked generating a backlash from the French public in proceeding with this case. Yet having proposed legislation for which there was little Member State appetite, it had little choice but to act on the complaint by a wildlife conservation non-governmental organisation that France was failing to fulfil its EU obligations. Whilst its job of Treaty guardianship would have been easier had the Commission built up a culture of institutional respect, such that it could work more through declaration and persuasion rather than coercion, that is not the position in which the Commission finds itself. That means forcing the pace nationally in respect of a 'laggard' Member State, even if the national public is not 'on side', and even if – returning to the Duich Moss case mentioned in the introduction to this chapter – national provisions are in place that have the same objectives.

The point is not that coercion is a weakness in regulatory law, but that it is a prerequisite in this field that it is underpinned by goodwill. Britain's domestic regulatory law takes at its starting point the goodwill of landlords and tenant farmers, and the important contribution of voluntary organisations bearing on the conservation side of estate management and farming, not so much in campaigning for law reform

---

[112] Case C-383/09 *Commission v France* [2011] ECR I-4869. The wild European Hamster (*Cricetus Cricetus*) is common in some Member States (Hungary, the Czech Republic, Slovakia, Romania), but it is threatened in France and Germany (and the Netherlands and Belgium). In France it is near to extinction, because of land-use planning decisions. France was found on Commission investigations of a complaint to have taken insufficient steps to protect the species from changes in agriculture and urbanisation that had little regard to their burrows.

[113] M Clement, 'Global Objectives and Scope of the Habitats Directive: What Does the Obligation of Result Mean in Practice?' in Born et al (eds), n 27, 9, 10.

[114] ibid 9.

[115] Kramer, n 3, 335.

but in doing the practical jobs of conservation, sometimes by acquiring the land to be conserved, at other times working with the consent of the proprietor. With this core of goodwill in place, it has been possible to develop over many decades an increasingly coercive regime in which it is a criminal offence to undertake potentially damaging operations set out in management agreements between proprietor and regulator. The main stages in this regulatory evolution are the Acts of 1968, 1981, 1991, 1995, 2000 and 2006.[116]

The question mark over EU competence in relation to Britain's habitats is highlighted by a selection of statistics about practical compliance with EU law, and also Britain compliance with wider international law, beginning with the percentage of its territory designated under the Natura 2000 paradigm. No EU Member States has less of a proportion of its territory designated under the Directive, prompting the CEO of one voluntary society to complain, 'In the UK there has been a narrow approach to the implementation; "do the minimum possible" has been the mantra.'[117] The terrestrial SACs in England number 242, compared to 4,126 SSSIs.[118] But 'minimum' in this context refers to sites of significance within the notion of 'EU heritage', rather than nationally or, crucially, internationally. All 4,000 of England's SSSIs engage the UN Biodiversity Convention.

Another illustration of the independence of Britain's SSSI system concerns the number of post-2016 referendum designations. Since the public voted to leave the EU, Britain's – and in particular England's – SSSI network has expanded considerably, thanks to two of the largest ever SSSIs to have been confirmed, one in the north and one in the south.[119] In the first quarter of 2018, Natural England notified four sites,

---

[116] Viz Countryside Act 1968 (s 15); Wildlife and Countryside Act 1981 (s 28 and s 29); Wildlife and Countryside (Amendment) Act 1991; Environment Act 1995 (s 62); Countryside and Rights of Way Act 2000, pt III, amending the Wildlife and Countryside Act 1981 s 28; Natural Environment and Rural Communities Act 2006. See S Payne, 'From Carrots to Sticks – Natural Habitat Protection After the Countryside and Rights of Way Act 2000' (2001) 13 *Environmental Law and Management* 238.

[117] M Shardlow, 'Habitats Directive – Imperfect, But Still the Best in the World', Buglife Blog, 22 May 2015, available at https://www.buglife.org.uk/blog/matt-shardlow-ceo/habitats-directive-imperfect-but-still-best-in-the-world.

[118] The pattern is broadly similar throughout Britain and Northern Ireland. Wales has 85 terrestrial SACs compared to 1,073 SSSIs; Scotland has 236 terrestrial SACs compared to 1,423 SSSIs; Northern Ireland has 57 SACs compared to 392 ASSIs.

[119] West Pennine Moor SSSI (confirmed in 2017, covering 7,600 ha, or 30 square miles); Mid Cornwall Moors SSSI (confirmed 2017, covering 1,650 ha).

adding a further 2,000 hectares to the network.[120] To put this expansion in the SSSI scheme in England in a judicial context, Neuberger LJ, in the *Trailers and Marinas* case, thought that the territory of England's SSSIs had peaked at 7 per cent.[121] The doctrinal importance of this in terms of interference with the applicant's property rights is to highlight the exceptional character of a SSSI designation, which helped the Government's argument that it was a proportionate interference with the applicant's rights to exploit land. With this latest designation activity, however, the territory covered by England's SSSIs is nudging 9 per cent. The gap in England's coverage compared to Wales (12 per cent) and Scotland (12.7 per cent) is slowly closing.

The more significant statistics relate to the condition of habitats as between SSSIs, on the one hand, and the wider Natura 2000 regime, on the other. Britain and the EU have very different targets for protected habitats being in good or recovering condition. The English one is for 95 per cent of habitats to be in 'favourable' or 'unfavourable but recovering' condition by 2020.[122] The current figure of 94 per cent of SSSIs is not far off, and compliance is a realistic prospect.[123] By contrast, the EU is a long way from meeting a much lower target of 34 per cent of habitats being favourable or improving by 2020. The European Environment Agency reports that, in 2001–06, 17 per cent of assessed EU habitats were in 'favourable' condition and 4 per cent 'unfavorable but improving'; in 2007–12 that has declined to 16 per cent 'favourable' with a stable 4 per cent 'improving'.[124] Natura 2000 habitats are seemingly in a considerably poorer state of health than the domestic habitats, and, like Kramer's *peau de chagrin*, the condition of these sites is declining. The prospect of the EU's complying with its international obligations is remote.[125]

---

[120] Langdon Ridge (345 ha); Poole Harbour (extension) (1,836 ha); Malvern Common (20ha); Lazy Meadow (4 ha): Natural England, 'New Notifications', available at https://consult.defra.gov.uk/consultation_finder/?sort_on=iconsultable_enddate&sort_order=ascending&advanced=1&tx=&st=open&au=&in=&de=.site.natural-england.

[121] *Trailer and Marina (Leven) Ltd v Secretary of State for the Environment* [2004] EWCA Civ 158 [11].

[122] United Kingdom of Great Britain and Northern Ireland, National Targets – Convention on Biological Diversity 1992, available at https://www.cbd.int/countries/targets/?country=gb.

[123] Natural England, 'Whole of England Reports', available at https://designatedsites.naturalengland.org.uk/ReportConditionSummary.aspx?SiteType=ALL.

[124] ibid 146.

[125] European Environment Agency, *State of Nature in the EU: Results from Reporting under the Nature Conservation Directives 2007–2012* (EEA 2015).

Yet whilst Britain seems to have arrested the substantial decline in the health of habitats over the period from the late 1950s through to the early 1990s,[126] Natural England reports that there is still work to do.[127] Territory under its jurisdiction that is in unsatisfactory condition comprises 37,000 hectares in an unfavourable condition with no improvement (3.46 per cent), 25,000 hectares that are unfavourable and declining (2.36 per cent), and 202 hectares that have been partially destroyed. Agriculture dominates the list of threats. The most common problem is overgrazing, accounting for the unsatisfactory condition of 11 per cent of the SSSIs (undergrazing is also significant),[128] followed by freshwater pollution, mostly from fertiliser run off (9 per cent). However, pesticides do not figure as prominently as their media profile would suggest: only one small site (5 hectares) is principally suffering under this strain. Furthermore, the data vindicate confidence in the planning system as able to weigh habitat conservation interests heavily enough in SSSIs.[129]

III. CONCLUSION

Habitat conservation is an especially challenging aspect of the EU environmental acquis. It is challenging both for the Commission, as Treaty guardian, and for a Member State like Britain, battling with the conflicting wishes to respect EU law and for exclusive national competence in this field. The pull of independence is based on the subject matter's links with the land, and the narratives of nationhood that crystallise around it. Unlike pollution of water and air, which deal with chemicals that are rather indifferent to nationhood, habitats (and the life they support) have an altogether more complex 'chemistry'. Focusing on Britain, the post-war narrative of habitat conservation through the lens of the countryside has lost little, if any, of its rich currency. A recent survey by the Peak District National Parks Authority suggests that there are 20 million visits a year, mainly by repeat visitors from the surrounding urban centres. As hoped by architects of the regime, these roughly reflect the

---

[126] National Audit Office, Protecting and Managing Sites of Special Scientific Interest, HC 379 (HMSO 1994); and Radcliffe, n 82. See also Rodgers, n 44, 114.

[127] Natural England, 'All of England Adverse Conditions', available at https://designatedsites.naturalengland.org.uk/ReportUnitAdverseCondition.aspx?ReportTitle=All%20of%20England%20adverse%20conditions.

[128] Accounting for 5% of the sites (ibid).

[129] In less than 1% of sites in unsatisfactory condition is this status owing to planning permission (eg for houses, peat extraction, minerals, landfill) (ibid).

'social composition' of Britain, with an intriguingly higher-than-average proportion from 'areas of deprivation' (55 per cent), but (at 5 per cent) a lower than average 'black and ethnic minority' (BME) social grouping.[130]

The Government clearly sees leaving the EU as an opportunity for intensification of the application of the voluntary principle. The 25 Year Plan envisages the introduction of conservation covenants for England and Wales, along similar lines to the 'conservation burdens' enacted in Scotland under the Title Conditions (Scotland) Act 2003.[131] Whilst agreements between proprietors and regulators, backed by payments from the latter to the former, have been a feature of the domestic law for many decades, a conservation covenant would add important nuance. The covenants envisaged in the 25-year Plan differ from management agreements under the current English and Welsh SSSI regime in that they are at the initiative of the proprietor (rather than, say, Natural England), and second, they include positive obligations to manage land for conservation purposes, rather than the emphasis on refraining from potentially damaging operations under the current English and Welsh regime. In this respect they are similar to settled land. What is interesting is that the 25-year Plan commits to addressing the decline in public investment in this field, because it has meant that Natural England has had to concentrate on its narrow regulatory functions, leaving no time to support broader voluntary initiatives.[132]

---

[130] Peak District National Park Authority, *Visitor Survey 2014 and Non-Visitor Survey 2014* (PDNA 2014), available at http://www.peakdistrict.gov.uk/__data/assets/pdf_file/0005/538772/vistor-non-visitor-survey-2014.pdf.

[131] HM Government: *A Green Future: 25 Year Plan for the Environment* (Crown Copyright 2018). Title Conditions (Scotland) Act 2003, ss 38–42. This would implement the recommendations of the Law Commission, *Conservation Covenants: Law Commission Paper No 439* (HC 322 2014).

[132] On the problem of incentivisation of voluntary initiatives (focusing on covenants), see B Holligan, 'Narratives of Capital versus Narratives of Community: Conservation Covenants and the Private Regulation of Land Use (2018) 30 *Journal of Environmental Law* 55, 59ff. To put this in perspective, Natural England's budget has fallen from £200m in 2006/07 to £112m in 2017/18: House of Lords Select Committee on the Natural Environment and Rural Communities Act 2006, *The Countryside at a Crossroads: Is the Natural Environment and Rural Communities Act 2006 Still Fit for Purpose?*, Report of Session 2017–2019, HL Paper 99 (Stationery Office 2018) [95]. The Committee highlights that this has meant that Natural England has not had the time or resources to support individuals and groups seeking 'informal' advice about habitat conservation.

7

Conclusion

I N THIS BOOK, I have attempted to critically examine a powerful claim
that has shaped much of the anxiety about Brexit, namely, that
Britain entered the EEC the 'dirty man of Europe'. The label, popu-
larised by Friends of the Earth in the early 1980s, was not intended as an
empirical claim. Rather, it operated rhetorically, to prick the conscience
of politicians (and regulators) who boasted of 'Britain's way', but who
did not work hard enough (in the Friends' opinion) on delivering it in
practice. I have argued that Friends of the Earth would not have existed
but for the British way ideal. It is precisely because of the power of the
ideal that the 'dirty man' motif was coined, and is a catalyst.

I have further argued that remaining in or leaving the EU is not a
choice between robust or weak environmental protection. The choice,
rather, is between environmental protection the British way and environmental protection with a mix of the British way and the laws and
institutions of the EU jurisdiction. My analysis leans towards the desirability of the British way independent of the EU, for four main reasons.

First, *simplicity*. Whilst leaving the EU involves a complicated legal
drafting exercise, unravelling the domestic from the EU regime, that is
nothing compared to the complications arising from their being together
in the first place. The current arrangement is complicated by parallel
regimes of national law relating to the environment: one originating in
Britain and one originating in the EU. This is strongly illustrated by all
the case studies, but perhaps most starkly by air quality. Here, nitrogen
dioxide and other pollutants are provided for under separate regimes
operating at different sub-national scales, with differences in terms of
flexibility and in respect of the attainment of common, health-based
objectives. Though the EU regime is more 'ambitious' in this field, as
others, that is not necessarily a better way to do environmental law than
one oriented around 'practical' goals that are deliverable.

Second, *accountability*. Environmental non-governmental organisations sometimes make a virtue out of the European Commission
not being accountable electorally. Songbirds in Southern Europe are

protected, so the reasoning goes, in a way that would not have been possible if the protection rested on national institutions answerable to vested national electoral interests, for example bird hunters (and consumers of bird products). But national electorates are sidestepped in this way at great risk of storing up constitutional problems 'down the line'. There is no better (general) reflection of this than the result of the 2016 referendum.

Third, *autonomy*. The internationalist socialist EP Thompson wrote polemically of the EEC regime in terms of 'beetles being bred by bureaucrats in Brussels to blight what remains of the our active democratic traditions'.[1] The introduction of qualified majority voting in environmental matters has compounded this problem, because it has opened up a situation in which a Member State, or minority group of them, can be required to fall in with the majority; they become, in effect, an instrument of the majority. In practice, EU actors usually show self-restraint, seeking a consensus, but the exception considered in this book – the Landfill Directive – proves the rule. The Directive has made Britain's favoured mode of disposal a more costly and challenging option than the country wishes.

Thompson's polemic is a reminder of how controversial was the principle of ceding some national sovereignty under the European Communities Act 1972, not only on the political left but across the political spectrum. It was accepted only by a slender majority of 309 to 301 MPs on the Bill's second reading in the House of Commons.[2] Many were unpersuaded by the Prime Minister's argument that the loss of sovereignty was a price worth paying for the economic gains arising from participation in a common market. Environmental protection played *no* part in the debate about Community entry. This lack of debate, or rather the lack of a compelling reason for Britain's being part of a common environmental policy and law, is the fourth main reason for leaning towards a clean break. In the debate about leaving or remaining in the EEC in 1975, all the reasoning in the environmental field was on the side of leaving. A clean break has *rationality*.

To capture the questionable rationality of the arrangement Britain is leaving as concisely as possible, in none of the case studies is there evidence that the domestic environment is well protected through the EU-originating aspect of domestic law. This comes back to Lord Diplock's

---

[1] EP Thompson, *Writing by Candlelight* (Merlin Press 1980) 87.
[2] For a concise and engaging discussion, see D Sandbrook, *State of Emergency: Britain 1970–1974* (Penguin 2010) 167–69.

question: 'Have you considered to what extent you wish to hand over environmental control to the institutions of the Community and the extent to which it is dealt with nationally?' The key thing here is the use of the present tense, to recognise that the environment *is* protected domestically. Why 'hand over', if only partly, to a new jurisdiction?

POSTSCRIPT

Section 16 of the European Union (Withdrawal) Act 2018 is a highly significant provision which was inserted into the Bill repealing the European Communities Act 1972 late in the Parliamentary process. It arose from an amendment tabled by Lord Krebs, a crossbench peer who is sympathetic to the Greener UK alliance's campaign to retain 'EU environmental protections'. That alliance was responsible for the section's wording. The upshot is that the Government must put before Parliament draft primary legislation consisting of a 'set of principles' to which the Government 'must have regard', viz:

–   the precautionary principle so far as relating to the environment,
–   the principle of preventative action to avert environmental damage,
–   the principle that environmental damage should as a priority be rectified at source,
–   the 'polluter pays' principle,
–   the principle of sustainable development,
–   the principle that environmental protection requirements must be integrated into the definition and implementation of policies and activities,
–   public access to environmental information,
–   public participation in environmental decision-making, and
–   access to justice in relation to environmental matters.[3]

What is the significance of this?

If, as seems inevitable, the Withdrawal Act is to be understood as having a constitutional status, within the parameters of Laws LJ's obiter dictum in *Thoburn*,[4] these principles will be constitutionally entrenched.

---

[3] European Union (Withdrawal) Act 2018, s 16(2).
[4] *Thoburn v Sunderland City Council* [2002] 3 WLR 247.

Thus, they not only obligate the executive (to initiate legislation) but are, if the constitutional statute analysis holds true, binding on future Parliaments at Westminster.[5] That is to say, legislation which is inconsistent with section 16 will only have force insofar as section 16 is explicitly repealed. This is not a revolution, but it is a radical step. It will ensure that domestic environmental law is made, adjudicated and enforced with more systematic regard to principles than at any time covered by the analysis in this book, including the period of EU membership. In that regard it is telling that, under the EU Treaty, these principles are addressed first and foremost to the EU institutions, not Member States.

To reinforce the sense of a new departure for the British way represented by section 16, not one of the 11 principles to which the Government must have regard originated in the EU or its Community predecessors; all are derivative. They derive from international agreements which Britain helped draft, and to which it will remain party. Whilst section 16, then, was clearly intended as a means of locking in a 'soft Brexit' environmentally, my understanding is that it is an encouraging expression of a twenty first century, independent British way of environmental protection.

---

[5] Whether it is both s 16 *and* future legislation passed under it that has (or is to have) 'constitutional status' is unclear. It does not matter in terms of the 11 principles which are entrenched in manner and form under the suggested constitutional status of the 2018 Act, but the question may arise for practical consideration should the implementing legislation add to the set of principles provided for in the 2018 Act. It is unclear that the provisions of s 16 regarding public authority enforcement are sufficiently precise for them to have 'constitutional status'.

Bibliography

Ashby, E, 'Between Brussels and Westminster', *Nature* (26 April 1984) 802.

—— and Anderson M, The Politics of Clean Air (Oxford University Press 1981).

—— et al, Pollution: Nuisance or Nemesis (HMSO 1972).

Ashworth, W, *The Genesis of Modern Town Planning* (Routledge 1954).

Ayers, P, *Shaping Ecology: The Life of Arthur Tansley* (Wiley-Blackwell 2012).

Badie, B and Birnbaum, P, *The Sociology of the State*, trans A Goldhammer (University of Chicago Press 1983).

Ball, S, 'Reforming the Law of Habitats Protection' in C Rodgers (ed), *Nature Conservation and Countryside Law* (University of Wales Press 1996) 85.

Barnes, J, Chatterton, T and Longhurst, J, 'Policy Disconnect: A Critical Review of UK Air Quality Regulation in Relation to EU and LAQM Responsibilities over the last 20 Years' (2018) 85 *Environmental Science and Policy* 28.

Barritt, E, 'Conceptualising Stewardship in Environmental Law' (2014) 26 *Journal of Environmental Law* 1.

Bate, R, 'Saving Our Streams: The Role of the Anglers Conservation Association in Protecting English and Welsh Rivers' (2003) 14 *Fordham Environmental Law Journal* 375.

Bevan, A, *In Place of Fear* (Simon and Schuster 1952).

Bigham, A, *The Law Relating to the Environment* (Oyez 1972).

Blandy, S, Bright, S and Nield, S, 'The Dynamics of Enduring Relationships of Property in Land' (2018) 81 *Modern Law Review* 85.

Bosselmann, K, 'Environmental and Human Rights in an Ethical Context' in L Kotze and A Grear (eds), *Research Handbook on Human Rights and the Environment* (Edward Elgar 2015) 531.

Bramwell, E, 'UK Government Policy' (1994) 3 *European Environmental Law Review* 44.

Brenner, J, 'Nuisance Law and the Industrial Revolution' (1973) 3 *Journal of Legal Studies* 4.

Brimblecombe, P, 'Attitudes and Responses Towards Air Pollution in Medieval England' (1976) 26 *Journal of the Air Pollution Control Association* 941.

——, *The Big Smoke: A History of Air Pollution in London Since Medieval Times* (Methuen 1986).

Bugler, J, *Polluting Britain: A Report* (Penguin 1972).

——, 'Friends of the Earth is 10 Years Old' *New Scientist* (30 April 1981) 294.

Burns, C, Gravey, V and Jordan, A, *UK Environmental Policy Post-Brexit: A Risk Assessment* (Friends of the Earth 2018).

Burton, T, 'Access to Environmental Information: The UK Experience of Water Registers' (1989) 1 *Journal of Environmental Law* 192.

Cahill, K, *Who Owns Britain and Ireland: The Hidden Facts Behind Landownership in the UK and Ireland* (Canongate 2001).

Cannadine. D, *GM Trevelyan: A Life in History* (Harper Collins 1992).

Casteleiro, A, 'EU Declarations of Competences in Multilateral Agreements: A Useful Reference Based?' (2012) 17 *European Foreign Affairs Review* 491.

Cavert, W, *The Smoke of London: Energy and Environment in the Early Modern City* Cambridge University Press 2016).

Cherry, G, *The Evolution of British Town Planning: A History of Town Planning in the United Kingdom During the 20th Century of the Royal Town Planning Institute, 1914–1974* (Leonard Hill Books 1974).

Clement, M, 'Global Objectives and Scope of the Habitats Directive: What Does the Obligation of Result Mean in Practice?' in C-H Born, A Cliquet, HJ Schoukens, D Misonne and G Van Hoorick (eds), *The Habitat Directive in its EU Environmental Law Context: European Nature's Best Hope?* (Routledge 2015).

Clapp, B, *Environmental History of Britain* (Longman 1994).

Cooper, T, 'Challenging the "Refuse Revolution": War, Waste and the Rediscovery of Recycling 1900–1950' (2008) 81 *Historical Research* 710.

——, 'War on Waste: The Politics of Recycling in Post-War Britain 1950–1975' (2009) 20 *Capitalism, Nature, Socialism* 53.

Cosgrove B, 'Throwaway Living: When Tossing Out Everything Was All the Rage' *Time Magazine* (15 May 2014).

Coyle, S and Morrow, K, *Philosophical Foundations of Environmental Law* (Hart Publishing 2004).

Davis, D, *When Smoke Ran Like Water* (Basic Books 2002).

Dicey AV, *Lectures on the Law and Public Opinion in England in the Nineteenth Century* (Macmillan 1906).

——, *Introduction to the Study of the Law of the Constitution*, 8th edn (Macmillan 1915).

Dingle, AE, 'The Monster Nuisance of All: Landowners, Alkali Manufactures and Air Pollution 1826–1864' (1982) 35 *Economic History Review* 529.

Elsom, D, *Atmospheric Pollution: Causes, Effects, Control Problems* (Basil Blackwell 1987).

European Environment Agency, *State of Nature in the EU: Results from Reporting under the Nature Conservation Directives 2007–2012* (EEA 2015).

——, Air Quality in Europe – 2017 Report (EEA 2017).

Fisher, E, Lange, B and Scotford, E, *Environmental Law: Text, Cases, and Materials* (Oxford University Press 2013).

Fisher, E, 'The Enigma of Expertise' (2016) 28 *Journal of Environmental Law* 551.

——, *Environmental Law: A Very Short Introduction* (Oxford University Press 2017) 122.

——, 'Back to Basics: Thinking About the Craft of Environmental Law Scholarship' in O Pedersen, *Perspectives on Environmental Law Scholarship* (Cambridge University Press 2018).

Forster, M, 'The Landfill Directive: How Will the UK Meet the Challenge?' (2000) 9 *European Environmental Law Review* 16.

France-Hudson. B, 'Surprisingly Social: Private Property and Environmental Management' (2017) 30 *Journal of Environmental Law* 101.

Garner, J, *The Public Control of Land* (Sweet & Maxwell 1959).

—— and Jones, B, *Countryside Law*, 3rd edn (Shaw and Sons 1997).

Garwood, C, 'Green Crusaders or Captives of Industry?: The British Alkali Inspectorate and the Ethics of Environmental Decision Making, 1864–95' (2004) 61 *Annals of Science* 99.

Gay, H, 'Before and After Silent Spring: From Chemical Pesticides to Biological Control and Integrated Pest Management, Britain 1945–1980' (2012) 59 *AMBIX* 88.

Girling, R, *Rubbish! Dirt on Our Hands and the Crisis Ahead* (Transworld Publishers 2005).

Girouard, M, *Hardwick Hall: A Brief Guide* (National Trust 1977).

——, *Life in the English Country House* (Yale University Press 1978).

——, *Return to Camelot: Chivalry and the English Gentleman* (Yale University Press 1981).

——, *A Country House Companion* (Yale University Press 1987).

Glinski, C and Rott, P, 'Waste Incineration – Legal Protection in European Environmental Law' (2000) 12 *Journal of Environmental Law* 129.

Goodhart, D, T*he Road to Somewhere: Populist Revolt and the Future of Politics* (C Hurst and Co 2017).

Gordon, S, *Down the Drain: Water, Pollution and Privatization* (Optima 1989).

Gotsova, B, 'EU's Procedure for Concluding International Treaties' (2015) 24 *European Energy and Environmental Law Review* 44.

Grant, M, *Urban Planning Law* (Sweet & Maxwell 1982).

Griffiths, JAG, 'The Political Constitution' (1979) 42 *Modern Law Review* 1.

Haigh, N, 'Environmental Quality Objectives in Britain: National Policy or Community Obligation', Working Paper (Institute of European Environmental Policy 1982).

——, *EEC Environmental Policy and Britain: An Essay and a Handbook* (ENDS Data Services 1984).

——, 'Devolved Responsibility and Centralization: Effects of EEC Environmental Policy' (1986) 64 *Public Administration* 197.

——, 'The European Community and International Environmental Policy' in A Hurrell and B Kingbury (eds), *The International Politics of the Environment* (Oxford University Press 1992) 230.

——, *EU Environmental Policy: Its Journey to the Centre Stage* (Routledge 2016).

——, *The Single Market and the Environment: What Kind of Access After Brexit?* (Institute of European Environmental Policy 2018).

—— and Baldock D, *Environmental Policy and 1992* (Institute of European Environmental Policy 1989).

Hamer, M, *Wheels Within Wheels: A Study of the Road Lobby* (Friends of the Earth 1974)

——, 'Ministers Opposed Action on Smog' *New Scientist* (5 January 1984).

Hawkins, K, *Environment and Enforcement: Regulation and the Social Definition of Pollution* (Oxford University Press 1984).

Hedemann-Robinson, M and Wilde, M, 'Towards a European Tort Law on the Environment? European Union Initiatives and Developments on Civil Liability in Respect of Environmental Harm' in J Lowry and R Edmunds (eds), *Environmental Protection and the Common Law* (Hart Publishing 2000) 201.

Hempen, S and Jager, F, 'Germany's New Waste Management Act – Towards the Management of Material Flows and Closed Substance Cycles' (1995) 4 *European Environmental Law Review* 138.

Hennessey, P, *Having it So Good: Britain in the Fifties* (Penguin 2007).

Hilson, C, 'The Impact of Brexit on the Environment: Exploring the Dynamics of a Complex Relationship' (2018) 7. *Transnational Environmental Law* 89.

Holdgate, M, *A Perspective of Environmental Pollution* (Cambridge University Press 1979).

——, Penguins and Mandarins (The Memoir Club 2003).

Holligan. B, 'Narratives of Capital versus Narratives of Community: Conservation Covenants and the Private Regulation of Land Use' (2018) 30 *Journal of Environmental Law* 55.

Horwitz. M, *Transformations in American Law*.

Howarth, W, *Water Quality Law* (Shaw and Sons 1987).

——, 'The History of Water Law in the Common Law Tradition' in T Tvedt, O McIntyre and T Woldetsadik (eds), *History of Water Series III: Sovereignty and International Water Law* (IB Tauris & Co Ltd 2014) 66.

Johnson, S, *The Politics of the Environment: The British Experience* (Tom Stacey 1972).

Kinnersley, D, *Troubled Water – Rivers, Politics and Pollution* (Hilary Shipman 1988).

Knill, C, *The Europeanisation of National Administrations* (Cambridge University Press 2001).

Kotze L, *Global Environmental Governance: Law and Regulation for the 21st Century* (Edward Elgar 2012)

Kramer L, 'Law in an Open Society' (1989) 1 *Journal of Environmental Law* 1.

——, *EEC Treaty and Environmental Protection* (Sweet & Maxwell 1990).

——, *Focus on European Environmental Law*, 2nd ed (Sweet & Maxwell 1997).

——, 'EU Environmental Law and Policy Over the Last 25 Years – Good or Bad for the UK?' (2013) 25 *Environmental Law and Management* 48.

——, 'Implementation and Enforcement of the Habitats Directive' in C-H Born, A Cliquet, HJ Schoukens, D Misonne and G Van Hoorick (eds), *The Habitat Directive in its EU Environmental Law Context: European Nature's Best Hope?* (Routledge 2015) 229.

Lamb, R, *Promising the Earth* (Routledge 1996).

Lange, B, 'The Emotional Element of Regulation' (2002) 29 *Journal of Law and Society* 197.

——, 'National Environmental Regulation? A Case Study of Waste Management in England and Germany' (1999) 11 *Journal of Environmental Law* 59.

Lee, M, *EU Environmental Law: Challenges, Change and Decision Making* (Hart Publishing 2005).

——, *Environmental Accountability After Brexit*, UCL European Institute Working Paper (UCL November 2017).

Lee, R, 'Always Keep a Hold of Nurse: British Environmental Law and Exit from the European Union' (2017) 29 Journal of Environmental Law 155.

—— and Small, L, *Waste Regulation Law* (Bloomsbury 2016).

Llewellyn, K, 'Law and the Social Sciences – Especially Sociology' (1949) 62 *Harvard Law Review* 1286.

—— and Hoebel, A, *The Cheyenne Way: Conflict and Case Law in Primitive Jurisprudence* (WS Hein and Co 1941).

Lobban, M, 'Tort Law, Regulation and River Pollution: The Rivers Pollution Prevention Act and its Implementation, 1876–1951' in T Arvind and J Steele (eds), *Tort Law and the Legislature: Common Law, Statute and the Dynamics of Legal Change* (Hart Publishing 2013) 329.

Locke, J, *Second Treatise on Government*, ed CB Macpherson (Hacket Publishing 1980).

Longhurst, J and Conlan, D, 'Changing Air Quality in the Greater Manchester Conurbation' (1970) 3 *Transactions on Ecology and the Environment* 349.

Loughlin, M, *The Idea of Public Law* (Oxford University Press 2003).

Lucy, W, 'Replacing Private Property: The Case for Stewardship' (1996) 55 *Cambridge Law Journal* 566.

Macdonald, H, 'In Search of Post-Brexit England, and Swans' *New York Times Magazine* (5 January 2017).

Macrory, R, 'Environmental Citizenship and the Law: Repairing the European Road' (1996) 8 *Journal of Environmental Law* 219.

—— and Newbigin J, 'The United Kingdom's International Obligations After Brexit' in O Fitzgerald and E Lein (eds), *Complexity's Embrace: The International Law Implications of Brexit* (McGill-Queens University Press 2018) 241.

—— and Thornton, J, 'An Environmentally Ambitious Brexit', *Demos Quarterly* (20 June 2017).

Malinauskaite, J, Jouhara, H, Spencer, N, 'Waste Prevention and Technologies in the Context of the EU Waste Framework Directive: Lost in Translation?' (2017) 26 *European Energy and Environmental Law Review* 66.

Marshall, B, 'German Attitudes to British Military Government' (1980) 15 *Journal of Contemporary History* 655.

McAuslan, P, *Ideologies of Planning Law* (Pergamon Press 1980).

——, 'The Role of Courts and Other Judicial Type Bodies in Environmental Management' (1991) 3 *Journal of Environmental Law* 195

McLaren, JPS, 'Nuisance Law and the Industrial Revolution – Some Lessons from Social History' (1983) 3 *Oxford Journal of Legal Studies* 155.

Mehta, A and Hawkins, K, 'Integrated Pollution Control and its Impact: Perspectives from Industry' (1998) 10 *Journal of Environmental Law* 61.

Merchant, C, *Autonomous Nature: Problems of Prediction and Control from Ancient Times to the Scientific Revolution* (Routledge 2015).

Morag-Levine, N, 'Is the Precautionary Principle a Civil Law Instrument? Lessons from the History of the Alkali Act' (2011) 23 *Journal of Environmental Law* 1.

More, N, 'Pesticides and Birds – A Review of the Current Situation in Great Britain 1965' (1965) 12 *Bird Study* 222.

Nicholson, M, *The Environmental Revolution: A Guide for the New Masters of the Earth* (Hodder & Stoughton 1970).

Osborn, D, 'Reflections on UK Environmental Policy, 1970–1995' (1997) 9 *Journal of Environmental Law* 1.

Payne, S, 'From Carrots to Sticks – Natural Habitat Protection After the Countryside and Rights of Way Act 2000' (2001) 13 *Environmental Law and Management* 238.

Pimlott, B, *Hugh Dalton: A Life* (Jonathan Cape 1985).

Pontin, B, 'Tort Law and Victorian Government Growth: The Historiographical Significance of Tort in the Shadow of Chemical Pollution and Factory Safety Regulation' (1998) 18 *Oxford Journal of Legal Studies* 661.

——, 'Nuisance Law and the Industrial Revolution: A Reinterpretation of Doctrine and Institutional Competence' (2012) 75 *Modern Law Review* 1010.

——, 'The Common Law Clean up of the "Workshop of the World": More Realism about Nuisance Law's Historic Achievements' (2013) 40 *Journal of Law and Society* 173.

——, *Nuisance Law and Environmental Protection: A Study of Injunctions in Practice* (Lawtext Publishing 2013).

——, 'Nuisance Law, Regulation and the Invention of Prototypical Pollution Abatement Technology: "Voluntarism" in Common Law and Regulation' in R Brownsword, E Scotford and K Yeung (eds), *Oxford Handbook of Law, Regulation and Technology* (Oxford University Press 2017) 1253.

Porter, E, *Water Management in England and Wales* (Cambridge University Press 1978).

Radcliffe, D, *The Nature Conservation Review*, vol 1: *The Selection of Biological Sites of National Importance to Nature Conservation in Great Britain* (Cambridge University Press 1977).

Rodgers, C, 'Planning and Nature Conservation: Law in the Service of Biodiversity' in C Miller (ed), *Planning an Environmental Protection* (Hart Publishing 2001) 91.

——, *The Law of Nature Conservation: Property, Environment and the Limits of Law* (Oxford University Press 2013).

Rose, C, *The Dirty Man of Europe: The Great British Pollution Scandal* (Simon and Schuster 1991).

Russell, E, *War and Nature: Fighting Humans and Insects with Chemicals* (Cambridge University Press 2001).

Sandbrook, D, *State of Emergency: The Way We Were – Britain 1970–1974* (Allen Lane 2010).

Sanderson. F et al, 'Assessing the Performance of EU Nature Legislation in Protecting Target Bird Species in an Era of Climate Change' (2016) 9 *Conservation Letters* 172.

Scruton, R, *Where We Are: The State of Britain Now* (Bloomsbury 2017).

Sheail. J, *An Environmental History of Twentieth-Century Britain* (Palgrave 2002).

Shoard, M, *Theft of the English Countryside* (Maurice Temple Smith Ltd 1980).

——, *Right to Roam* (Oxford University Press 1999).

Sijswick von, M, 'EC Water Law in Transition: The Challenge of Integration' [2003] 3 *Yearbook of European Environmental Law* 249.

Simms, B, *Britain's Europe: A Thousand Years of Conflict and Cooperation* (Allen Lane 2016).

——, 'The World After Brexit' *The New Statesman* (1 March 2017).

Squintani, L and Rakipi, J, 'Judicial Cooperation in Environmental Matters: Mapping National Courts Behaviour in Follow Up Cases' (2018) 20 *Environmental Law Review* 89.

Stevenson, D et al, *Organisation and Youth: 50 million Volunteers* (HMSO 1972).

Stokes, R, Koster, R and Sambrook, C, *Business of Waste: Great Britain and Germany, 1945–Present* (Cambridge University Press 2013).

Suykens, C, 'EU Water Quantity Management in International River Basin Districts: Crystal Clear?' (2015) 24 *European Energy and Environmental Law Review* 134.

Tansley, A, 'Nature Reserves and Nature Conservation' (1944) 13 *Journal of Ecology* 4.

——, *Britain's Green Mantle*, 2nd edn (Allen & Unwin 1968).

Tansley, A, *The British Islands and their Vegetation* (Cambridge University Press 1939).

Thomas, C, *Material Gains: Reclamation, Recycling and Re-Use* (Friends of the Earth 1974).

Thompson, FML, *English Landed Society in the Nineteenth Century* (Routledge 1971).

Thornton, J and Macrory, R, 'An Environmentally Ambitious Brexit', *Demos Quarterly* (20 June 2017).

Thorsheim, P, 'The Paradox of Smokeless Fuels: Gas, Coke and the Environment in Britain, 1813–1949' (2002) 8 *Environment and History* 381.

——, *Inventing Pollution: Coal, Smoke and Culture in Britain since 1800* (Ohio University Press 2006).

Trevelyan, GM, *Illustrated English Social History*, vol 4 (Longman 1952).

Tromans, S, 'EC Waste Law – A Complete Mess?' (2001) 13 *Journal of Environmental Law* 133.

Turing, HD, *Third Report on Pollution* (British Field Sports Society 1949).

Twining, W, *Karl Llewellyn and the American Legal Realist Movement*, 2nd edn (Cambridge University Press 2014).

Varvastian, S, 'Achieving the EU Air Policy Objectives in Due Time: A Reality or a Hoax?' (2015) 24 *European Energy and Environmental Law Review* 2.

Verney, RB et al, *Natural Resources: Sinews for Survival* (HMSO 1972).

Vogel, D, *National Styles of Regulation: Environmental Policy in Great Britain and the United States* (Ithaca, NY, 1986).

——, 'The Politics of Risk Regulation in Europe and the United States' [2003] 3 *Yearbook of European Environmental Law* 1.

Voulvoulis, N, 'EU Water Framework Directive: From Great Expectations to Problems of Implementation' (2017) 575 *Science of the Total Environment* 358.

Warren, L, 'Conservation – A Secondary Consideration' in R Churchill, L Warren and J Gibson (eds), *Law, Policy and the Environment* (Basil Blackwell 1991) 73.

Weale, A, 'Environmental Rule Making in the EU' (1996) 3 *Journal of European Public Policy* 594.

Weiner, M, *English Culture and the Decline of the Industrial Spirit, 1850–1980* (Cambridge University Press 1981).

Weston, B and Bollier, D, *Green Governance: Economics, Human Rights and the Law of the Commons* (Cambridge University Press 2013).

White, H, 'Fifty Years of Electrostatic Precipitation' (1957) 7 *Journal of the Air Pollution Control Association* 166.

Willers, M and Shirley, E, 'The Public Trust Doctrine's Role in Post Brexit Britain', *Garden Court Chambers Working Paper* (31 March 2017).

Williams, P, *Waste Treatment and Disposal* (Wiley 1998).

Wils, W, 'Subsidiarity and EU Environmental Policy: Taking People's Concern Seriously' (1994) 6 *Journal of Environmental Law* 85.

Wilson, AN, *After the Victorians 1901–1953* (Hutchinson 2010).

Wilson, GS, 'Farm Safety' (1966) 23 *British Journal of Industrial Medicine* 1.

Wincott, D, 'Images of Welfare in Law and Society: The British Welfare State in Comparative Perspective' (2011) 38 *Journal of Law and Society* 343.

Winter, G, 'Property Rights and Nature Conservation' in C-H Born, A Cliquet, H Schoukens, D Misonne and G Van Hoorick (eds), *The Habitat Directive in its EU Environmental Law Context: European Nature's Best Hope?* (Routledge 2015) 215.

Wood, M, *We Wore What We'd Got: Women's Clothes in World War II* (Warwickshire Books 1989).

Wurzel, R, *Environmental Policy-Making in Britain, Germany and the European Union* (Manchester University Press 2006).

Zweiniger Bargielowska. I, *Austerity in Britain: Rationing, Controls and Consumption, 1939–1955* (Oxford University Press 2000).

Index